BLACKSTONE'S
HANDBOOK FOR MAGISTRATES

BLACKSTONE'S HANDBOOK FOR MAGISTRATES

Neil McKittrick, LLM

A Stipendiary Magistrate for the Middlesex Area

Pauline M. Callow, JP, LLM

BLACKSTONE PRESS LIMITED

First published in Great Britain 1997 by Blackstone Press Limited,
9-15 Aldine Street, London W12 8AW. Telephone 0181-740 2277

ISBN: 1 85431 456 4

British Library Cataloguing in Publication Data
A CIP catalogue record for this book is available from the British Library

Typeset by Montage Studios Ltd, Tonbridge, Kent
Printed by Livesey Limited, Shrewsbury, Shropshire

Contents

Foreword
by The Rt. Hon. Lord Bingham

The task of trying those accused, and punishing those convicted, of breaking the rules which members of a community are bound to observe is one of the oldest and most fundamental functions of government. In different countries the task is handled in different, sometimes very different, ways.

In England and Wales there has evolved over the centuries a unique and invaluable solution: the recruitment of a body of part-time, unpaid, legally unqualified justices, reinforced in the great urban centres by a much smaller group of professional paid magistrates, who between them hear and decide the overwhelming majority of criminal cases.

It is a system which depends for its success on many things: the training which newly-appointed justices are now required to undergo; the quality of the legal advice which lay justices receive from their clerks; the balance and heterogeneity of local benches; and the efficiency with which the business of the courts is conducted. But above all the success of the system depends on the willingness of fair and independent-minded people to undertake the interesting and rewarding but exacting, responsible and time-consuming task of acting as justices, and on the willingness of such people to familiarise themselves with the powers and duties of magistrates' courts and the broad principles which should govern any exercise of judicial authority.

This book is just what its name suggests, a Handbook for Magistrates. It is addressed both to those seeking (or considering whether to seek) appointment and to those already appointed. There will be few, even in the ranks of long-serving justices, who will not find much to learn. The magistrates' courts are so central to our legal system, and are a democratic institution of such value, that anything which strengthens them is greatly to be welcomed; and I am confident this timely book will have that effect.

The Rt. Hon. Lord Bingham of Cornhill
Lord Chief Justice of England

Royal Courts of Justice
Strand WC2
24 February 1997

Preface

In writing this first edition of *Blackstone's Handbook for Magistrates*, we have sought to provide a wide-ranging account of the work of lay magistrates in England and Wales. The book is intended primarily for those who might be thinking about becoming magistrates, those who have recently been appointed, and magistrates in their first few years on the bench. We hope it will also be valuable as a reference book for more experienced magistrates, especially those whose responsibilities include training their less experienced colleagues.

The work of the magistrates' courts affects many others besides the magistrates themselves, and we hope the book will be of some interest to them too. Individual defendants and witnesses, and the general public whom the magistrates' courts serve, may find something worth reading. Likewise the professionals — probation officers, social services personnel, court legal advisors, the police, the Crown Prosecution Service and other prosecutors, newly qualified lawyers, and teachers, perhaps — may find some insights not easily available elsewhere.

Training courses for magistrates cover, in varying degrees of depth, a good proportion of what is said in this book, but we hope the book will prove a useful, permanent, and perhaps more comprehensive, source of reference. Other books for magistrates tend to concentrate on procedural and legal matters, but here we have tried to go beyond these, to give a flavour of what life as a magistrate is really like, touching on the pressures, responsibilities and rewards of the work. We have also sought to put the work of the magistrates into a wide context, for example, explaining the powers under which people are brought before the court in the first place, and linking what goes on in the magistrates' court to the court system as a whole and to certain broad principles on which the system of justice operates.

We examine how magistrates are appointed — a subject about which there are probably many misconceptions; what they are empowered to do; how their courts are organised and operated; the kinds of matters they deal with, such as criminal offences, traffic matters and civil work (notably in family matters); how they go about assessing evidence and deciding what to accept as true; how they decide whether defendants should be released on bail or kept in custody; the sentences they may impose and how they endeavour to make the punishment fit the crime. The popular press might have us believe that magistrates send people to prison with great frequency; in fact imprisonment is a sentence of last resort reserved for the most serious cases, and new magistrates soon come to realise that it is a rare outcome indeed. We also look at how legal aid works, which is a subject currently of general public and political concern. Last, but not least, we have tried to address some matters of concern to magistrates as individuals.

The book illustrates in detail the huge responsibility that lay magistrates take on their shoulders, and the fearsome consequences their decisions have on the people who come before them. It is no small matter for a person of hitherto unblemished character to face the possibility of being convicted of a criminal offence, or to have to await trial in prison rather than at liberty. It is a tribute to the diligence with which magistrates go about their tasks, and to the strenuous efforts of the Lord Chancellor's Department and the Magistrates' Association to promote consistent principles, that public criticism is relatively rare.

In writing the book, we have tried to say what we have to say in a straightforward way, avoiding legal terminology when it was sensible to do so, but the nature of the subject limits the scope for this. We hope we have succeeded in explaining legal terms satisfactorily.

The law is a dynamic subject and the criminal law in particular has been subject to many changes in recent years. For example, at the time of writing, the Criminal Procedure and Investigations Act 1996 has just been passed and will come into force at a time yet to be decided. The book was written during the summer of 1996 and, as far as the law is concerned, is up to date to 1 February 1997.

The authors will be glad to hear of any comments or suggestions for improvements in future editions of *Blackstone's Handbook for Magistrates*.

The authors take this opportunity to thank Robert Allan of Haringey Magistrates' Court for reading the final draft of the text and for his comments, help and encouragement; and Jim Stack of Brent Magistrates'

Court who reviewed an earlier version of the text. Finally, the forbearance of Alistair MacQueen and Heather Saward at Blackstone Press, who waited long and patiently for the typescript, must also be acknowledged.

One

Introduction

Background

It is well known that the office of justice of the peace or magistrate (the words are interchangeable for all practical purposes) can be traced back to before the fourteenth century; a statute of 1361 is still the source of certain powers of modern magistrates. Much has happened since those days of relatively primitive justice, but the disposal of the vast majority of criminal cases by people without special legal qualification, who are not paid for the work, remains unique in the world. Magistrates deal with something over 95 per cent of all criminal cases, and in almost all the remaining cases they have some role in the preliminary stages. This includes deciding whether a defendant will be released on bail pending the final outcome, and hearing committal proceedings with a view to deciding whether or not to send a case for trial at the Crown Court.

There are about 30,000 lay magistrates, serving in some 700 courts in England and Wales. About 1,800 new magistrates are appointed each year, to supplement numbers and replace those who retire. There are also about 100 professional or 'stipendiary' magistrates, who are legally qualified and paid a salary or 'stipend' (see also Chapter 4). They work mainly in the busier courts in major cities, and were first appointed in the eighteenth century, to deal with the increasing workload. Their numbers have increased slightly in recent years. Likewise, the number of lay magistrates increased by some 5 per cent between 1990 and 1994. Indeed, some years ago it was even suggested that non-legally qualified people might be appointed to deal with certain civil cases in the county courts — a radical proposal which has not borne fruit.

In the early days, magistrates were selected from the 'great and good', often the highest-ranking or wealthiest in society. The twentieth century has seen the introduction of a far broader-based magistracy. The idea now is that magistrates should be drawn from all sectors of society. While that is fine in theory, in reality individual commitments and circumstances still restrict the sphere of people from whom magistrates can be drawn. Although employers are, strictly, obliged to allow people time off work to serve as magistrates, there is no requirement to pay them. Advertising in newspapers and even on the sides of buses has helped to attract a wider range of people, but the system for nominating potential magistrates probably still favours certain types and militates against others. Work and domestic responsibilities will always be inhibiting factors. This is, however, an area in which women play a full part, 47 per cent of lay magistrates being women, and some areas having more women magistrates than men. On the other hand, the make-up of some benches of magistrates is said not fully to reflect the social and cultural mix of the populations they serve. It is estimated that 2 per cent of lay magistrates come from the cultural minorities.

Becoming a magistrate

Finding out

Most people never even give a thought to the possibility of becoming a magistrate. The system of magistrates' courts has probably passed them by, and any knowledge they may have results from reading about court cases in the local press. Becoming a magistrate could not be further from their minds. This is because of the image of the magistracy as aloof from ordinary folk, a repository of privilege, a self-perpetuating oligarchy, or, conceivably, a part-time job for which they are not remotely qualified. The magistracy itself must acknowledge the validity of this perception despite the fact that it is well wide of the mark, and despite the unstinting efforts of the Magistrates' Association to provide information as to who magistrates are and what they do.

The Lord Chancellor's Department provides explanatory leaflets and the clerk to the justices at the local magistrates' court will always assist with information, but the best way for a member of the public to get an insight into what magistrates do is to find out on what days the local court sits, and then go along and watch. All magistrates' courts are open to the public — justice in this country is administered openly — and all court rooms have seats (sometimes called 'the public gallery') where ordinary members of the public can go. The public is not allowed into youth courts, i.e., those dealing with children and young persons who have not attained their eighteenth birthdays; nor is the public allowed into family proceedings courts, where highly sensitive matters involving families and the welfare of children are heard. The reasons for keeping the public out of these sorts of court hearings are understandable.

Two or three visits to sit in the public gallery should give an excellent insight into what magistrates do, and the observer will also be able to identify the roles of others in court: the clerk to the court or legal advisor; the prosecution and defence advocates; witnesses; the probation officer; the press reporter; the defendant; court security officers and the usher. The role of the usher is a key one to assist the smooth running of the courts, and ushers are usually unfailingly helpful. Try to have a few words with the usher and explain that you have come along to observe proceedings. The usher may well be able to tell you what is coming up in the court session, and may give you a copy of the court list which will enable you to follow cases easily. Ushers have many jobs to do: informing the legal advisor which cases are ready; calling parties into court; swearing in witnesses; rounding up advocates who may have cases in other court rooms, and handing forms to the defendant and others involved in a case. Despite all these responsibilities, most will find time for those who are genuinely interested to know a little about how the court is run.

After a couple of visits, you will have an idea of whether the work is likely to be of interest. You may have seen some interesting cases, and others which are fairly routine, where traffic offenders have been fined in fairly quick succession for exceeding the speed limit, or something similar. The important thing to remember is that, although routine, these cases may be of some significance to the defendants concerned, and the bench will attach the same care to dealing with them as to other more 'high profile' cases. You will also have noted that no two cases are ever the same, similar perhaps, but not the same. If you think that serving the community in this way might interest you, you will wish to consider taking it further.

The commitment

However, there is no point going further unless your personal circumstances allow you to do it. Magistrates are unpaid and they are expected to perform a fair share of sittings on the bench. The precise number of sittings varies from bench to bench, but it is not unreasonable to assume that you must be prepared to give a minimum of one half-day per fortnight, and probably more. If you are in work, you will need to know whether your employer will grant you time off for magisterial duties. Many remain generous in this, but it might be worth having a private word with your boss to see whether time off is likely to be a problem. You will already know whether your personal circumstances are such as to enable you to devote time to bench sittings and to training, which is such a developing feature of magisterial life. If you know someone who is already a magistrate, make contact and find out more. If not, try to speak to the chief executive or clerk to the justices at your local court. As a bare minimum, he or she will be able to give you an application form and is likely to give further assistance.

The Lord Chancellor's Department and the local advisory committees

Magistrates are appointed by the Lord Chancellor who does so on behalf of the Queen. The Lord Chancellor is a political appointee, a member of the cabinet, who is the Government's spokesman on legal affairs in the House of Lords. He also has numerous ceremonial functions. The Lord Chancellor's Department runs the court system and the administration of justice as a whole, while the Home Secretary is responsible for the police, probation and prison services, and policy and legislation in matters of criminal law.

In practice, the Lord Chancellor appoints magistrates on the advice of local advisory committees. The Lord Chancellor appoints the members of the committee — most are magistrates — and liaises closely with them. The advisory committees may in turn appoint subcommittees. The proceedings of all these committees are confidential; indeed until 1992 even the names of the members of the advisory committees were confidential.

For historical reasons, in Greater Manchester, Merseyside and Lancashire, appointments are made by the Chancellor of the Duchy of Lancaster, not by the Lord Chancellor, but the principles which apply are the same throughout England and Wales.

The application

A person can apply to be a magistrate of his or her own initiative, or may be recommended by another person (perhaps someone who is already a magistrate), or by an organisation (for example, by an employer who has been approached by the Lord Chancellor's Department with a view to finding new candidates). The procedure is begun by completing a form supplied by the local advisory committee or by the clerk to the justices at the local court. The form is usually accompanied by notes on the criteria for selection and on what is expected of those who are appointed. Prospective candidates can find out the address of the appropriate advisory committee from the local magistrates' court.

Apart from personal details about the applicant, the application forms may ask for details of any community work undertaken, general interests and political views (although, as mentioned on page 7, these have no bearing on the merit of an individual application). There are usually questions designed to identify candidates who may be ineligible on the formal grounds discussed below. Candidates are also asked to name two referees, from whom the advisory committee may later seek written references. Referees should not be related to the candidate, and may be an employer, a professional colleague, an existing magistrate, a local councillor, or other person who can say something relevant to the candidate's suitability.

A completed application form will probably be acknowledged, but that may be all the applicant will hear for some months. This is a regular feature of the process, and has nothing to do with the merits of the individual application.

Qualifying

There are certain formal rules about who may be appointed. For example, a prospective magistrate must normally live or work in the area in which he or she will serve, and must be medically fit to perform the duties of a magistrate. The candidate must also be able and willing to undertake a normal allocation of work. What is 'normal' varies from area to area, depending on the overall workload and number of magistrates available to deal with it, but the expectation is that magistrates will attend at least 26 times a year, an attendance being a half-day, and that their attendance will be spread fairly evenly over the year. In practice, however, many magistrates sit twice as often as the minimum.

Certain persons are ineligible to be considered for the magistracy. These are:

— those over the age of 60 unless there are exceptional circumstances; as a rule, younger candidates (those in their thirties and forties) are preferred;

— those who have been convicted of certain offences or are subject to certain court orders;

— undischarged bankrupts;

— those who are not medically fit for the duties of a magistrate, for example someone whose sight or hearing is impaired;

— serving members of Her Majesty's forces, members of the police service and traffic wardens;

— close relatives of a person already on the same bench.

All those matters are fairly straightforward. The critical requirement for appointment to the magistracy is that a person must be of suitable character, integrity and understanding. It is a matter for the advisory committee to decide, on the basis of a completed application form, references and interview, whether these criteria are met.

The selection process

In some areas, candidates are seen twice. The first occasion may consist of a meeting of a group of prospective magistrates, perhaps observing court proceedings then discussing them with the magistrates concerned and the legal advisor. There may be a talk to explain basic principles and eliminate misconceptions about what is involved. A prospective candidate who is put off by a preliminary meeting of this kind, or decides he or she would not take to the work, may decide at this stage to proceed no further.

The second meeting — or, in areas where a single-stage selection procedure operates, the only meeting — takes the form of an interview with the individual candidate, designed to assess his or her suitability, i.e., whether he or she is 'magistrate material', that is to say, open-minded, able to listen to argument and reason on what has been said, and to proceed to a decision. The experience may seem fairly daunting, particularly to those unaccustomed to modern interviewing techniques. Some simple exercises may be given to assist the assessment. Interviewees should probably expect questions of the 'name three adjectives your friends and family might use to describe you' variety; and fairly close questioning about motives for applying, and about whether there is anything in the candidate's personal background which might make him or her unsuitable — the 'skeleton in the cupboard' question. There may also be questions designed to elicit judicial aptitude, for example, would the candidate argue for a lower sentence because he or she believed the defendant was not guilty, when the majority view was that the defendant was guilty? (Sometimes a bench of three magistrates has to reach a decision by a two-to-one majority, and, as will be apparent from reading Chapter 9, dissent on the question of guilt is not a valid consideration in deciding the sentence.)

Since it is for the advisory committee to make recommendations for appointment to the Lord Chancellor, the question of suitability is entirely in the committee's discretion. Those of us who are not in the know can only speculate about whether or not other independent investigation of a candidate's background is also undertaken.

All these matters apart, people will be recommended for appointment only if they are needed. Thus, if there are only four vacancies, only four people will be appointed even though more may be suitable. It is regrettable that some excellent candidates have been lost because of these rules.

In making appointments, advisory committees also have to seek to balance the political complexion of the bench and the numbers of men and women, and to reflect the local community in terms of ethnic mix and other factors. An individual's political views are not in themselves a determining factor, but are taken into account to seek a balance of views between the members of the bench overall.

Following the interview, more time will pass before, eventually, the applicant receives a letter explaining that the Lord Chancellor proposes to appoint the applicant as a magistrate, and seeking undertakings as to ability to carry out training and to perform a fair share of magisterial duties; or rejecting the application.

'Swearing-in'

On being appointed, a new magistrate is 'sworn in' before a judge. Usually, all new magistrates appointed at the same time to the same bench are sworn in together, perhaps at the court where they will sit or at the Crown Court for the area. Present at the ceremony, apart from the judge, will be the chairmen of the relevant benches, clerks to the justices, as well as one or two of each of the new magistrates' nearest and dearest.

Incidentally, the term 'bench' is used variously to refer to all the magistrates in a particular area, the magistrates sitting in a particular case, and the piece of furniture on which they sit (although chairs are fairly readily available these days!).

The substance of the swearing-in is the oath of allegiance and the judicial oath. These may be made on the holy book relevant to the person's religious belief ('I swear by Almighty God ...', for example) or by affirmation ('I do solemnly, sincerely and truly declare and affirm ...'). Both forms carry equal weight and no stigma attaches to those who do not espouse an organised religion.

The oath of allegiance is that the person making it 'will be faithful and bear true allegiance to Her Majesty Queen Elizabeth the Second, her heirs and successors, according to law'. And the judicial oath: 'I will well and truly serve our Sovereign Lady, Queen Elizabeth the Second, in the office of Justice of the Peace and I will do right to all manner of people after the laws and usages of this Realm without fear or favour, affection or ill-will'. The language is archaic, but the last sentence is at the heart of the work of the magistrate; that he or she will do justice in accordance with the law, regardless of any fear of the consequences or any improper influence. The oaths take only a few seconds to recite but the significance of them, and what is said generally, will last through the magistrate's career.

After all the new magistrates have taken the oaths, the judge will say a few appropriate words which emphasise the importance of the occasion, stressing the doing of justice in accordance with the oaths taken, and the serious obligation of doing justice to one's fellow citizens. This sounds almost insufferably formal. There is a formal side to it, but most swearing-in ceremonies mix the formal and the informal, and the formal proceedings may be followed by a small social gathering between the new magistrates, the judge, and officers of the court.

Initial training

New magistrates undertake initial training before they first sit in court. This usually comprises a certain number of sessions observing proceedings in court. The observations are conducted in a structured way, with the opportunity for the observer to join the adjudicating magistrates for a briefing from the legal advisor before the sitting, and then going into the retiring room at the end of the session so that any points that arose during the hearing can be explained. At any hearing, the time spent before going into court is invaluable. The legal advisor can advise on potentially troublesome points that may arise, and although the bench will have to decide on them having heard them argued in open court, the fact of having been alerted is helpful. Forewarned is forearmed. Similarly, whatever the seniority of the magistrates on the bench, there is great merit in spending a few minutes after the hearing to assess how the proceedings went. At all levels, magistrates are learning, developing skills, and will wish to improve their performance. Although at the end of the sitting there is often pressure to get back to work or to go home, a few minutes of discussion on how the business of the court went and how problems were dealt with is well worth it.

During their first year, magistrates also usually visit a number of penal institutions — prisons, youth custody centres and detention centres. In recent years the amount of training which magistrates must undergo has increased considerably, and serving magistrates must meet certain target numbers of hours' training. More about this is said in Chapter 3.

First sitting

A magistrate's first sitting can be slightly disconcerting, although some will be less fazed by it than others. You may be sitting with magistrates and a legal advisor whom you have not met before, but usually all magistrates sitting on the day will arrive at court 15 or 20 minutes early, so there will be an opportunity for introductions, and the legal advisor should help by explaining, before going into court, what kinds of cases are to be dealt with, and whether any are likely to pose any particular problems. Initial training will have provided a background, but many magistrates feel that however good that initial training, it is not until they actually start to take part in hearing cases that things begin to fall into place. The views of all magistrates on a bench, whether they have 30 minutes' or 30 years' experience, are of equal importance. A new magistrate — indeed a magistrate of any number of years' experience — can always ask the chairman to explain anything which is not immediately clear, or seek advice from the legal advisor.

The important thing is to remember that you have been appointed because it is felt that you are a suitable person to do justice in this place, and the words of the judicial oath are your judicial birth certificate. The learning curve is a steep one in the early years, but if the magistrate goes through periods of doubt about the value of the work to the community, he or she should go back and look carefully at those words. If the magistrate always tries to fulfil the obligation in the oath, it is difficult to go far wrong. The aim must always be justice, according to the law. That may sometimes be unpalatable, particularly where the law does not reflect what is seen to be the broader justice of the case, but such instances are rare. The law can be a surprisingly flexible companion, and the discretion vested in magistrates can be surprisingly wide.

Magistrates must remember, however, that they are not legislators, nor are they social workers. They do not make law, they apply it; and it follows that they must apply the law *as it is*, not as they would wish it to be. Nor are they there to 'help people'. It is to be hoped that some of the decisions they take will help people, particularly where the balance of the argument is that a rehabilitative sentence is called for, but while one hopes that a just application of the law may help people, that is not the purpose of the magistracy. Often a decision will have to made which will be aimed at balancing the interests of the offender before the bench and those of the wider and unseen public outside.

Who can I turn to?

Things are much better for the new magistrate now than in years gone by. Many new magistrates used to be told to turn up at court after the most perfunctory training and start to sit on the bench. In some cases (if rumour is to be believed), they were told to say nothing for five years! Nowadays, the chairman of the bench and the clerk to the justices will do their best to make the new magistrate feel swiftly at ease. Many benches have adopted the idea of giving each new magistrate a 'minder' — an experienced magistrate who will be their first port of call to deal with any queries that might arise.

The new magistrate will have met those sworn in at the same time. They become 'the year of '88' or 'the year of '95' or whatever, and their training will be undertaken together. Many magistrates appointed together become fast friends. The chairman of the bench will always help, and will not prove to be the austere figure the new magistrate may have feared. Chairmen cannot do enough to ensure their benches run smoothly, and the sooner new magistrates are made to feel at home, the better.

The clerk to the justices, apart from having responsibilities for the management of the court, is also the legal advisor to the magistrates, jointly and individually. He or she can always be consulted about a whole range of matters relating to the magistrate's duties. The clerk should be treated as a *confidant(e)*, and you will soon get to know the clerk, the deputy, and the rest of the legal team. You will probably not get to know other members of the staff of the court, apart from the ushers, but it is as well that the new magistrate realises that the clerk to the justices is head of a staff of administrative and financial officers who are there to prepare cases for court, give effect to decisions made in court, and collect fines, costs, compensation and maintenance ordered by the court. Their work is outside the magistrate's domain, and is rather unsung, but without their contributions, the magistrates' courts would not be able to function.

The duties of a magistrate

Magistrates usually sit in court as a bench of three. They can sit in pairs, although this carries the risk that they may not be able to reach agreement, which could lead to a case having to be tried again later by different magistrates. A single magistrate can decide certain matters alone.

Magistrates always have the services of a legal advisor, or clerk as they are still commonly known. All court legal advisors are qualified in law; some are solicitors or barristers; others have a Diploma in Magisterial Law.

The magistrates make decisions about disputed facts — did this defendant hit this police officer in the back? They must then apply the law — did what happened amount to an assault? Perhaps the defendant was in a crowd of people, stumbled, and crashed into the back of the officer. If so, this was not an assault since the defendant did not have the necessary intention. In applying the law, the court's legal advisor will explain and interpret the requirements. Thus, to constitute assault, the defendant must have the unlawful intention of striking the other person. The way the magistrates come to their decisions is the subject of Chapter 10.

If a person pleads guilty or is found guilty, the court must then impose a sentence, ranging from absolute discharge to imprisonment. Sentencing is dealt with in detail in Chapter 9.

Two types of cases, 'summary offences' and certain 'either way' offences, are dealt with entirely in the magistrates' courts. There is also a third category, 'indictable only' offences. Summary offences are the least serious and must be dealt with by the magistrates. 'Indictable only' offences are at the other end of the scale of seriousness and are heard at the Crown Court only, although, as we shall see, the magistrates have a role in the preliminary stages. 'Either way' offences are in between in terms of seriousness. As the name suggests, they can be tried in either the magistrates' courts or the Crown Court. Where they are dealt with depends on whether or not the magistrates decide the case is suitable to be tried by them and on the defendant's choice. This is dealt with in more detail in Chapter 5.

The kinds of cases dealt with by a particular court vary enormously. Sometimes the reasons are obvious. There will be more cases of soliciting and kerb-crawling in an area with an active red-light district than in one without. Magistrates in areas without motorways will not come across many cases of motorway offences. Football hooliganism generally occurs in and around football grounds, and if there is no stadium in an area, there will be few, if any, such cases. Cases of defrauding the Department of Social Security (DSS) may well increase if the DSS steps up investigations and prosecutions. Prosecutions for, say, car theft, may increase if the police decide to target this type of crime. Theft of livestock is confined largely to rural areas, while mugging, shoplifting and drug offences may be more prevalent in inner city areas characterised by social deprivation and unemployment. Motoring offences, however, make up a large part of all magistrates' work. In 1993, the police took action on 7 million motoring offences, and 2.4 million of these came to court.

Magistrates also deal with certain non-criminal matters, notably family cases and liquor licensing. Family cases mostly concern orders to make maintenance payments, and matters under the Children Act, including emergency protection orders, care orders, and orders for contact between a parent and a child. Here the people appearing in court will be representatives of the local authority, parents and other relatives of the child or children concerned, and sometimes even the child. As will be seen in Chapter 7, the approach to family court work differs in many respects from the approach to criminal court work.

Magistrates also have the unenviable tasks of dealing with council tax defaulters, non-payment of TV licences and road fund licences, and bus and train fare dodgers. They also have powers to authorise gas and electricity companies to enter buildings to cut off supplies for non-payment. And again, they may have to deal with cases brought by the local authority under legislation designed to protect consumers — food safety matters and trade descriptions, for example. There are also cases on environmental matters, such as pollution of waterways or excessive smoke emissions, which may be brought by the local authority or by the Environment Agency (formerly the National Rivers Authority and Her Majesty's Inspectorate of Pollution). All in all, this is a wide remit and most magistrates would agree that there are rarely two days the same.

The Magistrates' Association

The Magistrates' Association was founded in 1920 and provides a range of training programmes, some organised locally, others nationally. The great advantage of training events organised by the Association is that they give those attending the opportunity to compare notes with members of other benches, who may have quite different perspectives. The Association has 58 local branches. It publishes the journal *The Magistrate* and has a library which is open to members. All magistrates may join the Association on payment of an annual fee, currently £20. It has an office in central London, employing a small, full time staff. The Association is consulted frequently by government departments, particularly the Lord Chancellor's Department, and is uniquely placed to represent the views of magistrates.

The cost of the system

Finally, before leaving this introductory chapter, something about the costs of the system may be interesting. According to Home Office figures, public expenditure on the criminal justice system in 1993/94 was just under £9.5 billion. This compares with almost £23 billion spent on defence; £35.7 billion on health; and £30 billion on education.

Of the £9 billion spent on the criminal justice system, 64 per cent went on the police; 16 per cent on prisons; 8 per cent on the Lord Chancellor's Department; 5 per cent on the probation service; a mere 4 per cent on the magistrates' courts; and 3 per cent on the Crown Prosecution Service.

It is estimated that in 1993/94 the average cost of a prosecution was between £2,000 and £3,000 for an indictable offence and £200 to £300 for a summary offence. The average cost of a sentence is estimated at between £1,500 to £2,000 for an indictable offence, and zero for a summary offence. Custodial sentences are said to cost nearly 20 times as much as community service or probation orders.

In addition to these costs is the cost of legal aid. The total legal aid bill for 1994/95 was £1.4 billion, about one third of which was spent on criminal cases.

Two

The Court System

Introduction

What place does the magistrates' court occupy in the hierarchy of courts in England and Wales? In this chapter it is sought to put the work of the magistrates' courts into the context of the legal system as a whole, by looking first at the structure of the courts, and then at the sources of English law.

Criminal and civil cases

Broadly speaking, the courts can be divided into two groups, namely civil and criminal, although there is overlap, largely as a result of historical accident.

Criminal courts deal with people who are prosecuted, usually by the Crown Prosecution Service on behalf of the state, for behaviour which amounts to a crime. If the person pleads guilty or is found guilty, he or she is punished by the court on behalf of society as a whole.

Civil cases, on the other hand, usually arise out of disputes about rights and duties under the huge body of civil law. In most cases, the person bringing the case (usually called the 'plaintiff') hopes, at the end of it, to receive money or some other form of compensation from the person being sued, i.e. the 'defendant'. For example, a printer might sue a publisher for not paying bills for printing books. A patient whose surgery has failed might sue the surgeon for professional negligence. A private householder might sue a builder who made the leaking roof worse instead of better. Somebody who falls over a loose flag on a badly maintained pavement may sue the local authority for compensation for the injury caused. A petition for divorce and the proceedings concerning the children and maintenance are civil matters. So too are matters of landlord and tenant — a landlord seeking to remove a tenant may have to go to court for an order. Disputes about wills likewise may find their way to the civil courts.

The parties in civil cases may be private individuals, companies and other types of corporations and government departments.

Sometimes, cases overlap. A person convicted of falsely claiming social security benefits (a crime) may also be sued in a civil court for recovery of the money.

An important difference between criminal and civil cases is that in criminal cases, the prosecutor has to prove the case 'beyond reasonable doubt'; in civil cases, the person bringing the case must prove it on the less stringent 'balance of probabilities' test. More is said about these tests of proof on pages 154 and 156.

Almost all criminal cases start in the magistrates' courts and over 95 per cent of them are dealt with entirely in those courts. The remainder are referred by the magistrates' courts up to the Crown Court by a process called 'committal'. This is explained in Chapter 5. Magistrates' courts also deal with some civil matters, notably matters under the Children Act 1989, although these cases can also begin in the civil courts.

Where a civil matter begins is not quite so straightforward, but broadly, relatively simple cases involving smaller amounts of money begin in the county court; those which are more complex and feature claims for larger sums begin in the High Court.

Trial by jury

In the Crown Court, trial is by judge and jury, the jury making decisions on facts, the judge making decisions on points of law. The judge also has the task of controlling the trial — deciding, for instance, whether the rules of evidence allow a particular matter to be put to the jury, summing up the evidence, and directing the jury on its duties.

Since the majority of criminal cases are dealt with entirely in the magistrates' courts, it is immediately apparent that, despite what popular culture may suggest to the contrary, and despite public debate about whether the tradition of trial by jury remains relevant and likely to deliver justice, juries deal with only a tiny proportion of cases, although they include the most serious.

Appeals

Central to the concept of justice in English law is the freedom of a person in legal proceedings to appeal against a decision which the person believes to have been wrong. In criminal cases a defendant may appeal against the fact that he or she was convicted; or the defendant may accept that the conviction was correct but appeal against the sentence imposed. There are now also a few, strictly limited, possibilities for the prosecutor to appeal against certain decisions. The reason the prosecutor's freedom to appeal is severely restricted is the rule against double jeopardy — the tradition that a person should not be tried twice for the same offence. This long-established rule is designed to avoid oppression and bad faith.

In civil proceedings, any party may appeal against an award of compensation or against a judge's decision not to award compensation; or against any of a host of other orders and decisions that may be made.

Rights of appeal are subject to a variety of rules, including time limits, and in some circumstances the leave of the court is necessary before an appeal can be brought.

Appeals against convictions for criminal offences and appeals against sentences imposed by magistrates' courts are dealt with by the Crown Court, where they are heard by a Crown Court judge sitting with two magistrates (see Chapter 4 for the role of the magistrate in the Crown Court). But appeals based on a point of law only go to the Divisional Court of the Queen's Bench Division of the High Court. Appeals from the Crown Court go up to the Criminal Division of the Court of Appeal, and, if there is a further appeal after that, to the House of Lords. Appeals against decisions made in civil matters by the magistrates go to the High Court, usually the Family Division. Appeals from the High Court go to the Civil Division of the Court of Appeal and then on to the House of Lords.

Appeals from both county courts and the High Court are dealt with by the Civil Division of the Court of Appeal, and any further appeal would again be heard by the House of Lords.

Thus, at the bottom of the hierarchy are the magistrates' courts and the county courts; at the top is the House of Lords, and in between, the Crown Court, the High Court and the Court of Appeal.

The adversarial system

The English trial process — and this applies to both criminal and civil trials — is of an 'adversarial' or 'accusatorial' nature. In a criminal case, the prosecution builds up a case against the defendant, presents that case in court, and it is then for the defendant to deconstruct the case. This compares with the 'inquisitorial' system, widely adopted elsewhere in Europe. In France, for example, extensive independent investigations are conducted by a professional examining magistrate (*juge d'instruction*) before a decision is made about whether or not to prosecute. The examining magistrate has wide powers to interview witnesses, and is in control of the police investigation. He or she gradually builds up a picture of the suspect, his or her background and the circumstances of the incident, and then decides whether or not charges should be brought, and if so what charges. When a suspect is charged with an offence, the examining magistrate withdraws from the case. The role of the examining magistrate — the pursuit of the truth — is far more neutral than that of anyone concerned in the pre-trial procedures under the English system.

By contrast, the police investigating a case here are motivated by, for example, the need to find the perpetrator of an offence and to make out a convincing case. The Crown Prosecution Service decides whether or not to pursue a case according to a number of published criteria, notably the likelihood of success and whether or not it is in the public interest to do so. There are many arguments about the advantages and disadvantages of the two approaches, which probably need not be aired here. But one consequence of an adversarial system is that the fate of a suspect depends almost entirely on what happens on the day of trial.

The county court

As has been seen, the county courts deal with a great many cases based on a broad range of civil matters. These cases are heard and decided by county court judges and the more junior district judges. Again, if a matter comes to trial, the adversarial approach applies, the plaintiff presenting all the evidence and arguments that can be mustered in favour of the case, the defendant seeking to strike them down. In civil cases, though, there is plenty of scope for extensive pre-trial negotiations between the parties. These often produce some kind of compromise so that the court case can be dropped. Indeed, many cases are settled 'at the door of the court', the parties deciding that a last-minute compromise is better than risking going into court and losing.

The county courts also provide the 'small claims court' service, for cases where the sum of money involved is less than £3,000. A simplified procedure applies, the idea being that individuals can bring small cases themselves without having to employ solicitors.

The High Court

The judges of the High Court are appointed, on the invitation of the Lord Chancellor, almost entirely from experienced barristers, although solicitors are now also eligible for appointment. The system for appointment is informal and based largely on information about individuals garnered by existing judges and senior barristers.

The High Court is divided into the Queen's Bench Division, the Family Division and the Chancery Division.

The Queen's Bench Division is the busiest and deals with most disputes which are too large or complex for the county courts. It has an important subdivision called the Divisional Court which deals with appeals from magistrates' courts on matters of law. It also has powers of 'judicial review' with regard to decisions of government departments, local authorities and others. In recent years there has been an increase in the number of cases in which decisions, including certain high-profile decisions of cabinet ministers, have been struck down on judicial review. This may be because the judiciary is increasingly robust in its attitude, or because people are more willing to challenge official decisions, or because officials have increasingly misinterpreted or misapplied the law and laid themselves open to criticism. Whatever the reasons may be, the process of judicial review has proved increasingly popular — and effective — in recent years.

The Commercial Court, as its name suggests, deals with commercial cases, and the Admiralty Court with shipping matters. Both fall within the Queen's Bench Division.

The Family Division deals with divorce, maintenance and the division of money and other assets between divorcing and separating couples, and has all manner of tasks in relation to the welfare of children. It is also responsible for granting probate and letters of administration so that the affairs of a deceased person can be wound up.

Finally, the Chancery Division receives cases on financial matters, trusts, taxation and land.

The Court of Appeal and the House of Lords

Moving up to the Court of Appeal, this is, as we have seen, rather more logically divided into the Criminal and Civil Divisions, each dealing with cases of the appropriate category. The judges of the Court of Appeal, known as Lords Justices of Appeal, are selected from the ablest High Court judges.

Finally, appeals which get as far as the House of Lords are heard by five of the judges appointed from the members of the House of Lords to do so. An appeal cannot be made to the House of Lords unless the Court of Appeal or the House of Lords gives consent; consent is not usually forthcoming unless the case involves a point of law of particular public importance.

The European Court

Above all these courts there is now the Court of Justice of the European Communities ('the European Court') which sits in Luxembourg. It has the final word on all matters of EC law, and although this rarely extends to criminal matters, it is important in civil matters, notably commercial interests in connection with trade and competition.

The European Court of Human Rights

Quite separate from the European Court of Justice is the European Court of Human Rights which sits in Strasbourg and which was established under the European Convention on Human Rights. The Convention was negotiated and agreed at the instigation of the Council of Europe. This is nothing to do with the European Union, but is an international, intergovernmental organisation which seeks to protect human rights and democracy. It was a decision of the European Court of Human Rights which led to the now general precaution that a person at risk of imprisonment for non-payment of the community charge (poll tax) should be offered the opportunity to seek legal advice before a final decision is made (see pages 176–77). More recently, it has ruled that defaulters at risk of imprisonment should be entitled to legal aid.

Other ways of settling disputes

Finally, it may be worth noting that in civil matters a number of other mechanisms exist to settle, or to seek to settle, disputes. These may be preferred because they are cheaper or less confrontational than the courts, or because they bring special skills to resolving conflict. For example:

— arbitration. People entering into a contract may agree in advance that if any dispute arises it will be settled by arbitration. The contract may go on to specify how the arbitrator — usually a person with special knowledge of the subject matter of the contract — would be appointed. This is commonly done in building contracts and the travel trade, and is increasingly favoured in many other areas;

— industrial tribunals deal with claims under employment protection legislation — for unfair dismissal, for example;

— a great many other tribunals exist to deal with particular matters such as social security benefits, immigration and mental health cases;

— certain professional bodies, such as the Law Society, the General Medical Council and the General Dental Council, have their own tribunals to deal with disciplinary matters;

— many bodies provide mediation in cases of marriage breakdown, in an endeavour to help spouses find agreement rather than take a dispute to court;

— other methods of 'alternative dispute resolution'.

The sources of law

One of the great fascinations of the law is that it reflects history, politics, economics and changing social values. Politicians come and go; public concerns fluctuate with remarkable speed; theories of behaviour developed by sociologists and criminologists find favour then fade; moral values differ from individual to individual, but the law is the formal code by which society chooses to regulate its behaviour. For example, the Public Order Act 1986 strengthened the provisions on crimes of racial hatred in response to public concern about the increase in such incidents. The Police and Criminal Evidence Act 1984 gave suspects greater rights and imposed on the police a raft of duties designed to ensure the fair treatment of suspects. In the civil law, liberalisation of the divorce laws and the abortion laws illustrates that the law is a formal regulatory code and does not necessarily coincide with individual views about morality or the stability of social structures.

More immediately, our laws come from two sources: legislation and the common law.

Legislation

Much of our law derives from specific legislation — Acts of Parliament proposed, debated, and amended in the Houses of Commons and Lords and finally accorded Royal Assent by the Sovereign. During the 1990s there has been much new legislation in the field of criminal law, some of it motivated by a wish to make long-term improvements to the quality of justice, some motivated by short-term political expediency. For example, the short-lived unit fine system, introduced by the Criminal Justice Act 1991, proved disastrous and the Government was forced to backtrack very quickly. The same Act severely restricted the extent to which offenders' records could be taken into account when sentencing, and again this had to be abandoned very soon after. This is not to say that the 1991 Act was without merit; in Chapter 9, it is noted that this Act also introduced a structured approach to sentencing which has proved largely successful.

Acts of Parliament are increasingly supplemented by rules made by Statutory Instrument ('Regulations' or 'Orders'). Thus, an Act may lay down legal principles, but give authority to a particular government minister to make rules, having the force of law, on secondary matters such as procedure or dates of implementation. For example, the Children Act 1989 set out the 'welfare of the child', 'delay' and 'no order' principles, the orders which courts can make, and so on (see Chapter 7), but left many details to be filled in by Statutory Instruments. Thus, procedure, the court in which proceedings should start, fees payable and many other matters are regulated by a host of Orders and Regulations, which are amended and updated from time to time. These Regulations are drafted by government departments and become law by being laid before Parliament for the requisite period. They may be subject to 'positive' or 'negative' resolution; either Parliament must specifically approve them before they become law, or they become law in the absence of any objection. The latter is the more common method, although it has attracted some criticism as more and more matters are controlled by Statutory Instrument and are not subject to full Parliamentary scrutiny.

Local authorities may also be given powers to make by-laws applying in their own areas only. For example, the procedure by which local authorities can require dog-walkers to 'poop scoop' has just been vastly simplified in an attempt to make it easier to keep public places clean and hygienic.

The common law

Unlike many other countries, English law has not been fully codified into statute, and many important provisions do not appear in any written law, but remain based, wholly or partly, in the common law — established custom as adopted and developed by judges over the years. For the details of this kind of law, it is necessary to refer to reported judgments. The most important example of a common law offence is murder: the constituents of 'malice aforethought' and an intention unlawfully to kill or cause grievous bodily harm derive from what judges have said in the past, not from any Act of Parliament which says that murder is a crime. Statute has, though, intervened to impose a mandatory life sentence for those convicted of murder, and, more recently, to abolish the old common law rule that death must occur within a year and a day to constitute murder.

Precedent

In the interests of fostering certainty, the principle of legal precedent promotes consistency in decision-making. Thus, largely, higher courts should follow their own earlier decisions, and decisions made in higher courts are binding on lower courts: what the House of Lords says is binding on the Court of Appeal; what the Court of Appeal says applies in all lower courts. The principle of precedent applies to both civil and criminal cases, and to the interpretation of both common law and statute-based law.

Magistrates' courts and the Crown Court are not bound by their own earlier decisions, although, as we shall see, strenuous efforts are made to try to ensure consistency in sentencing. But they are bound by the decisions of the higher courts. Sometimes, earlier cases will be referred to in court, perhaps to illustrate what has in the past been taken to amount to a 'special reason' for not disqualifying a driver who would otherwise be disqualified automatically.

The tradition is to name criminal cases in the style '*R* v *Smith*', where *R* stands for *Regina*, all cases still strictly being brought by the prosecutor on behalf of the Sovereign; and *Smith* being the name of the defendant; or, for short, the case may be referred to simply as '*Smith*'. Reports published in the official law reports, the All England Law Reports and the Weekly Law Reports may well be mentioned.

Judicial interpretation

Although English legislation tends to be drafted in a fairly detailed way by comparison with that of other European countries, and certainly compared with European Community (EC) legislation, the draftsmen cannot always contemplate every conceivable situation, and are not always as precise in their wording as might be desirable. Gaps, inconsistencies and ambiguities are dealt with by 'judicial interpretation' in individual cases. Sometimes such interpretations reveal gaping holes in the law — tax lawyers are adept at seeking out such loopholes. Sometimes a court will refer to *Hansard* to clarify the intention of Parliament in passing a particular piece of legislation, in an endeavour to interpret it in the right spirit. Interpretations of this kind are, like everything else, subject to the rule of precedent.

Some judges have been said to be rather too imaginative in the use of this power, to the extent, some say, that they make law in usurpation of the prerogative of Parliament.

European Community law

Finally, the courts of England and Wales are subject to EC law, which takes priority over all domestic law. The Community makes laws by means of Directives (which must then be implemented in each member state by domestic legislation); Regulations (which are directly binding on the member states) and Decisions, which concern particular matters and are addressed only to the individual member state concerned. The system of law-making, in which the 15-member Commission, which is not directly elected, has the greatest say, continues to be controversial. Most of the EC's legislative activities do not affect the criminal courts, but environmental protection is an increasingly important exception. For example, and this is by no means an isolated example, Regulations which came into force in September 1996 implemented a directive on hazardous waste and created certain new criminal offences.

Text books

Text books have no formal place in making and interpreting the law, but advocates in court often refer to certain established works when seeking to persuade the judge of a particular point of view. Arguments on doubtful points of law are fairly rare in the magistrates' courts, but leading books are often referred to to explain the relevant law, even though it may not be in doubt. This is particularly likely in a case which is relatively unusual for magistrates. Among authoritative books some-times referred to are *Archbold (Criminal Pleading)*, *Blackstone's (Blackstone's Criminal Practice)*, *Stones (Stone's Justices' Manual)* and *Wilkinson (Wilkinson's Road Traffic Offences)*. Generally, the more editions of a book that have been published, and the fact that it is referred to by its author's (or original author's) name alone, the more authoritative it is!

The Law Commission

Again although it is not a direct source of law, it is worth mentioning the work of the Law Commission. This is a body of authoritative lawyers drawn from all walks of legal life who undertake extensive reviews of particular areas of law and make recommendations for improvement, clarification, simplification, amendment, restatement or even abolition. The Commission is highly respected in legal circles, and, for example, in the 1980s it produced detailed proposals for codifying the criminal law, although, as has been the case with many other well researched and carefully presented proposals of the Commission, Parliamentary time was not devoted to it and it has not been acted on.

Royal Commissions

Royal Commissions may also influence how law is made. Royal Commissions are appointed on an *ad hoc* basis by Government to investigate specific matters and make recommendations, but again, their advice is not always taken. For example, the 1993 Royal Commission on Criminal Justice recommended certain measures to restrict a defendant's right to trial by jury; these have not been adopted. Again, although a Royal Commission recommended no change to an accused person's right to silence, the law was nevertheless changed by the Criminal Justice and Public Order Act 1994 to allow a court, in certain circumstances, to draw an adverse inference from a defendant's failure to explain himself or herself.

Three

The Organisation of the Magistrates' Courts

Facilities

Like most other publicly-provided buildings, courthouses vary enormously, from the architecturally elegant to the downright scruffy. They may house a single court or two dozen, as well as offices for the administrative staff, cells, a reception area, interview rooms, a public gallery and magistrates' retiring room(s).

Court rooms also come in a wide variety of shapes, sizes and standards of comfort. But common to them all is that the magistrates sit at one end, usually on a raised platform, often beneath the Royal Arms. In front of them and usually a little below, facing in the same direction as the magistrates, sits the legal advisor. Facing the magistrates and the legal advisor are seats and desks for the lawyers; the prosecutor and the defence lawyer usually take the front row, those waiting their turn sitting behind.

Behind them, or perhaps to the side, is accommodation for the public, generally known as the 'public gallery' although in some cases that may be a rather grandiose term for the accommodation actually provided. Almost all proceedings in magistrates' courts (with the notable exceptions of family cases and youth court cases) are open to the public, for justice must not only be done, it must be seen to be done. We have already noted that prospective new magistrates can make use of the public gallery for their preliminary observations of proceedings. There may be a separate place for representatives of the press, or they may have to take their chances in the public gallery.

To the right and left are the witness box, the dock, and a place for the probation officer of the day to sit. In 'secure' courts, the dock leads directly to the cells, and cases concerning defendants in custody are usually allocated to these courts. Other courts may not have direct access to the cells, and are generally used for cases involving defendants on bail and for cases where imprisonment is unlikely to be the final outcome.

In the family proceedings court and the youth court the physical arrangements are less formal. In the family court, the emphasis is on the welfare of the child, and arrangements which less reflect the 'adversarial' approach are preferable. Likewise in the youth court, where care and treatment are primary considerations, a less formidable appearance is conducive to those purposes. Some court houses have court rooms specifically designed and furnished as youth courts and family courts; elsewhere, it is a question of moving the furniture around before the session begins.

Security

Until recently, police officers and prison staff were responsible for security in courts and for transporting defendants in custody between prison and the court. These functions have now been contracted out to private security firms. At first, much publicity was given to the number of prisoners 'lost' en route by the security companies (although, on reflection it seems that the reports tended to omit comparisons with how many had been mislaid under the old system!). In any event, this exercise in privatisation seems to have been fairly satisfactory. Prisoners are now brought into the dock by private security officers, and most courts will sit with a security officer present. In the — fortunately rare — event of having forcibly to remove someone from the court room for disruption or other contempt, the task falls to the security officer.

Magistrates who wish to view the cells, reception area and other 'front of house' facilities can usually arrange to do so by asking a member of the court staff.

Retiring rooms

Again, retiring rooms, and the standards of comfort they offer, vary. Some court houses have a separate retiring room behind each court;

others have a single retiring room which is used by all the magistrates. Whether the retiring room has five stars or none, this is the place where the magistrates deliberate, discuss and reach decisions. Here also, the legal advisor will often run through the day's list of cases with the magistrates before the court starts to sit, pointing out any which might present particular difficulty or prove particularly interesting. It is an inexplicable fact of life that magistrates tend to be particularly voluble, and this may be distracting in a shared retiring room, but in the absence of anything better, it simply has to be tolerated. The consolation is that it is becoming more and more common to provide a quiet place, however small, for reading pre-sentence reports, papers in family cases and so on.

The retiring room also has a more general function as a meeting place. All sorts of social activities may be organised. Notice boards announce training courses, rota vacancies, reports of appeals, dates of meetings, sports fixtures and so on. Friendships may be made and lost here. Getting to know other magistrates on the same bench may take some time, given that the rota system may mean seeing a particular person only once or twice a year, but is valuable in that it eases discussing cases, especially expressing differences of opinion.

The legal advisors

As noted in Chapter 1, magistrates always sit in court with a legal advisor (or clerk, the terms are interchangeable). Each petty sessional division has a clerk to the justices, who has overall responsibility for advising the magistrates on the law. Sometimes, the justices' clerk is also responsible for the management and administration of the court, in which case he or she may have the title 'clerk to the justices and chief executive', although in some areas there is a separate chief executive. Whether or not these functions should be divided between two persons has been the subject of some controversy. On the one hand, it is said that because the clerk to the justices must give wholly disinterested advice on the law, independent of considerations such as budgetary constraints or difficulties about court listings, the two posts should be separate. Indeed, the Police and Magistrates' Courts Act 1994 provides that in giving advice, a justices' clerk 'shall not be subject to the direction of the magistrates' courts committee, the justices' chief executive or any other person'. On the other hand, it is said that the overall administration of the system is best run by those thoroughly familiar with how the courts operate in practice

— an argument similar to that raised in criticism of the introduction of non-medically qualified managers in the National Health Service.

There are about 230 clerks to the justices, and each is assisted by a number of other legal advisors or 'clerks'. Justices' clerks are fully qualified solicitors or barristers. So too are many of the more junior legal advisors; others hold a Diploma in Magisterial Law or some other appropriate professional qualification.

Most justices' clerks belong to the Justices' Clerks' Society, a long-established and respected body which represents their professional interests and provides a forum for consultation among themselves and with the Government and other agencies. Other legal advisors and court staff may be members of the Association of Magisterial Officers.

Justices' clerks are appointed by the magistrates' court committee (see page 38), and appointment is subject to the approval of the Lord Chancellor. Other legal advisors are appointed directly by the committee.

The principal function of the legal advisor, *vis-à-vis* the lay magistrates, is to advise on the law. The magistrates may themselves seek advice. Since the system of justice should be as open as possible, it is as well to ask questions openly in court unless there is a particular reason for confidentiality. Thus, the chairman of the magistrates may ask the legal advisor 'What are our powers of sentencing for this offence?' or 'Please recap the elements of this offence'. But if the bench is considering disposing of a case in a particular and perhaps unusual way, and wishes to check it has power to do so, it may not wish to prejudice its final decision by saying publicly what it has in mind. Thus, although it is preferable to avoid whispered conversations between advisor and magistrates, this may have to be resorted to for a question like 'We are thinking of deferring sentence for six months; do we need the defendant's consent?'

The legal advisor may also give advice of his or her own initiative. For example, if there is a decided case which the advisor considers relevant to the case in hand, and it has not been mentioned by either the prosecutor or the defendant, the legal advisor may bring it to the attention of the magistrates, and will do so in open court in case either side wishes, say, to argue that that decision is in fact not relevant. Likewise, the legal advisor may intervene if the magistrates are going wrong, as where, for instance, they have misunderstood something which has been said. It is no disgrace, but rather a confirmation of the strength of the system, for a chairman to have to say something like, 'The bench is corrected. The defendant is indeed entitled to make a new application for bail'.

Interaction between the bench and the legal advisor reflects that the role of the legal advisor is confined to matters of law, and decisions are the sole province of the bench. For this reason, the legal advisor does not retire with the magistrates unless invited to do so. It is good practice, when retiring, for the chairman of the magistrates, if he or she thinks they will need the help of the legal advisor, to ask the advisor to accompany the justices to advise on any points of law which may arise.

Unfortunately for them, legal advisors also have to be available outside court hours, to advise on, say, an application for an emergency protection order made directly to a magistrate at home in the evening.

Because the workings of the court should be as self-evident as possible, it is sometimes said that the magistrates, and others in court, should address the legal advisor as 'Mister/Madam legal advisor'. Some may find this too cumbersome and artificial, and may prefer plain 'Mr Smith' or 'Mrs Jones', specifically explaining who the legal advisor is to anyone directly involved to whom it may not be obvious.

The legal advisors also play an important role in advising defendants who do not have lawyers, explaining the procedure and, perhaps, that what they have said amounts in law to a defence and that they should consider changing their plea from guilty to not guilty. Magistrates have been heard to remark that a defendant may fare better with the help of a court legal advisor than with certain lawyers!

The legal advisors also make notes of evidence, record who is present and what is decided, write up bail notices and perform a range of administrative duties, for example to arrange for the Driver and Vehicle Licensing Agency in Swansea to provide a 'printout' of a driver's record in a case adjourned for that purpose.

The clerk to the justices shares certain functions with the magistrates. These have increased in recent years and now broadly equate with what a single justice is empowered to do. Thus, the justices' clerk can adjourn cases, extend bail and grant legal aid (see Chapter 4) and may delegate this work to his or her staff.

The ushers

It has been noted in Chapter 1 that the court ushers occupy a unique place 'at the sharp end'. It is they who record the arrival of defendants, witnesses and lawyers; tell defendants where they can find the duty solicitor and supplement the posted court lists by telling people in which courts their cases will be heard. They, together with the lawyers, often have to take the brunt of the anger, frustration, disappointment and distress of defendants and witnesses. Sometimes they even have to act as baby-sitters for those who have not been able to find someone to look after a child while they come to court. The ushers are normally the only people in the magistrates' court to wear a gown.

The ushers usually decide the order in which to bring on the cases (although they can be overruled by the bench), checking which are ready to go ahead, and which defendants are still talking to their lawyers. Often they so manage things that all the cases in which a particular solicitor is involved are heard in sequence so that the solicitor can finish his or her court work for the day and go back to the office. They may also arrange for work to be switched between the courts to which it was originally allocated; perhaps Court 1's list has turned out to be shorter than expected but Court 2 is overloaded, so the usher, in consultation with the legal advisors, will bring some of Court 2's work into Court 1. Transferring cases in this way may also be necessary if a magistrate has to disqualify himself or herself from a case (see page 184), perhaps because he or she knows the defendant in some personal or professional capacity.

The ushers also have a host of other tasks in ensuring the courts work as smoothly as possible — photocopying documents, checking what trial dates are available and so on. In their 'spare time' when the courts are not sitting or have finished early, they are often deployed helping with general administrative work in the offices.

Administration

The justices' clerks, the other legal advisors and the administrative staff, besides their duties in court, also carry out a range of 'backroom' duties, including:

—   recording payments of fines and arranging for defaulters to be brought to court;

—   collecting maintenance payments under orders made in family proceedings, and passing the money to those entitled to it;

—   collecting money due under fixed penalty notices issued in road traffic matters (see Chapter 6);

—   organising the magistrates' timetable;

—   organising training for magistrates and staff;

—   preparing the lists for each court day, making sure the files are complete and ready;

— following up after a case has been in court — sending out adjournment notices, for example;

— processing legal aid applications (see Chapter 11).

The lawyers

Lawyers in England and Wales come in two different kinds, namely solicitors, and barristers or counsel. This is a curious division which contrasts with the situation in many other countries which have only a single variety of lawyer: the *avocat* in France; the *rechtsanwalt* in Germany; the *advocaat* in the Netherlands; the *abogado* in Spain.

The reason we have two branches of the legal profession here is largely historical, and although proposals to fuse the two professions have now largely been abandoned, the differences are little by little being eroded. For example, until 1990, only barristers had the right to conduct cases in the higher courts, including the Crown Court, but solicitors may now qualify to do so. It used to be said that the principal difference between the two professions is that barristers are specialists and solicitors are generalists. That remains true to some extent, and many barristers act as senior consultants on highly specialised areas of law, spending much of their time researching cases referred by solicitors and providing 'opinions'. But they do not train specifically for a particular specialisation; they are generalists when first 'called to the bar' on qualification, and specialisation tends to emerge over the years. But that said, many solicitors now specialise more and more, particularly as new areas of law develop. Proceedings to secure compensation for personal injuries, for example, are burgeoning and the body of law has developed considerably; some solicitors have followed these developments and have become specialists in this area. Environmental law likewise is relatively new, but, prompted to some degree by legislation emanating from the European Union, has grown enormously and many solicitors are settling into this niche.

A barrister of a certain number of years' experience may 'take silk' (having the privilege of wearing a silk rather than a stuff gown), becoming a Queen's Counsel (QC). Selection is by the Lord Chancellor in consultation with advisors in his department and at the bar. Taking silk usually leads to increased status and the possibility of later being appointed a High Court judge; it may also produce an increase in earnings. All barristers who are not silks are juniors, no matter how old they are, although experienced juniors are sometimes referred to, rather contrarily, as 'senior juniors'. Usually, a silk does not appear in court unless assisted by a junior.

The only common element in the training for each profession is that both study the same body of law. Thereafter, the barrister's life is characterised by a number of antique customs that need not concern us here, other than to note that in the magistrates' courts they do not wear their wigs and gowns. Although there has been some liberalisation of barristers' practices, an ordinary person still cannot consult a barrister directly, but must do so through a solicitor. The document in which a solicitor refers a case to a barrister, or 'instructs' the barrister, is called a brief, hence the expression, 'I want to see my brief'!

Most solicitors deal with a great variety of work. Thus High Street firms comprising perhaps two or three qualified solicitors are usually general practitioners, undertaking domestic and commercial conveyancing; writing wills and winding up estates; advising and conducting proceedings in divorce and other family matters; advising on disputes in civil cases (see Chapter 2); drawing up contracts; and many other matters. In larger firms, notably big city firms, some having more than 100 partners, individual solicitors tend to specialise in particular areas, e.g., shipping, trusts, company mergers, commercial contracts and so on. Many spend most of their time in their offices and rarely venture within the precincts of a court of any kind. But a large proportion of ordinary solicitors undertake criminal work and deal with a case from start to finish.

Solicitors may work on their own, in which case they are 'sole practitioners' and self-employed; or in partnership with others in which case they share office accommodation, facilities and fees; or they may be employed by a firm of solicitors or in the legal department of a commercial organisation, receiving a salary rather than a share in the fee income. Barristers, on the other hand, may not operate in partnerships and they work independently, although by tradition they usually group together in a 'set', sharing offices, or 'chambers'. For historical reasons, barristers each belong to one of the four Inns of Court, namely Gray's Inn, Lincoln's Inn, Middle Temple and Inner Temple. Barristers are represented collectively by the Bar Council.

Barristers operate on what is known as the 'cab rank principle' which means exactly what it suggests — they take the case which is at the head of the queue, provided the barrister is available and the subject is one with which the barrister is familiar. They may not first examine the prospects of success because the idea is to ensure that every person accused of an offence, particularly the distasteful offences such as rape or child abuse, can have the services of a lawyer.

One of the criticisms of the system is that a barrister often does not receive a brief until the last minute, perhaps only hours before the case comes on in court. This is usually because the barrister originally briefed has been detained by another case going on longer than expected, with the result that the brief is returned to chambers to be reallocated to another barrister. This is doubly frustrating for the client who may feel he or she is having to accept second best (although that may well not be so), and who may not meet their barrister until just before the case is called on in court.

In truth, whether the lawyer in court happens to be a barrister or solicitor is not terribly important in the day-to-day business of the magistrates' courts. Magistrates listening to lawyers may not even know whether they are solicitor or counsel, and it matters little. Many lawyers are good, some are indifferent and a few are plain bad. What does matter to magistrates is that they should not let their decisions be influenced by the fact that a lawyer may be irritating, condescending, unduly provocative, pompous, or, on the other hand, ingratiating, eloquent, courteous or especially fluent — none of these in itself has anything to do with the defendant's culpability or the heinousness of the crime.

Many solicitors deal with their clients' cases throughout, from first meeting the client through to sentence. But they may instruct counsel to deal with court appearances, either because they think counsel is better equipped to do so, or because they do not have the manpower to do it themselves. QCs rarely appear in the magistrates' courts, their expensive services generally being reserved for serious cases in the Crown Court and appeals to the Court of Appeal.

In cases brought by local authorities, for example prosecutions under food safety or trade descriptions legislation, a lawyer employed by the local authority may appear to present the case, or an outside solicitor or counsel may have been instructed. The same applies to cases brought by HM Customs and Excise and the Department of Social Security.

And finally on the subject of lawyers, they do tend to use language which sometimes seems rather quaint. They often refer to other lawyers as 'my friend' even though they are on opposite sides of the case. They may say, 'are you quite sure you are remembering that correctly?', implying, 'that doesn't make sense', or 'that contradicts what Officer So-and-So said'; or they may say, 'I put it you that you were at the Dog and Duck on Thursday evening' rather than, 'you cannot possibly be right in saying you were at home at the time'. These ways of putting things, which may at first seem rather strained and indirect, derive from tradition and conventions of courtesy, avoiding direct confrontation. It rapidly becomes clear to new magistrates that they do not in fact detract from the force of what the lawyer is saying.

The Crown Prosecution Service (CPS)

Until 1986, prosecutions were conducted by the police. The main objection to this was that it was not in the interests of fairness that the police, who are responsible for investigating alleged crimes, should also have the conduct of the prosecution. As long ago as 1929 a Royal Commission said that it was important to separate 'on the one hand, the duty that lies on the police of preventing and detecting crime, and, on the other, the duty of bringing to justice people who have broken the law'. There was also considerable variation in practice between the 43 police forces in England and Wales, and an excess of weak cases coming before the courts. In the interests of independence, and of consistency and certainty in practice, an independent prosecuting body was desirable. This finally led to the establishment, in 1986, of the Crown Prosecution Service (CPS).

The CPS is based in over 100 offices throughout England and Wales and employs about 6,000 staff, over one third of whom are barristers or solicitors. The Director of Public Prosecutions (DPP) is the head of the service; although politically neutral, the DPP is accountable to the Attorney General. The offices of DPP and Attorney General are of much more ancient origin than the CPS, the first DPP having been appointed in 1880. The present DPP is Dame Barbara Mills QC. She may herself prosecute a case if it is particularly difficult or of exceptional importance.

The CPS handles some 1.5 million cases a year. It is responsible for prosecuting all criminal offences, except traffic offences in respect of which it is possible to plead guilty by post. Also outside the CPS's remit are cases of serious or complex fraud, which are handled by the Director of the Serious Fraud Office; there is a special procedure for these cases to commence in the Crown Court without first coming before the magistrates' court. The magistrates therefore take no part in these intriguing and challenging cases.

Even if the CPS decides not to prosecute a case, there is no reason why an individual cannot bring a private prosecution, and this does sometimes happen, although doing so may well require exceptional application and perseverance. The prior consent of the DPP is required before bringing a prosecution for certain unusual offences, including incest and aiding and abetting suicide and riot, none of which is the common stuff of the magistrates' courts. The CPS may take over a prosecution begun privately. It is noted elsewhere that certain cases are brought by local authorities, the Department of Social Security and HM Customs and Excise, but the CPS prosecutes the vast majority.

Having investigated a case, collected evidence and identified a suspect, the police charge the suspect. They may consult the CPS before bringing the charge. The file is then sent to the CPS which reviews the case to decide whether or not to proceed to prosecute the offence charged, or a different offence, or additional offences. The CPS is not obliged to bring a prosecution simply because a person has been charged.

The decision whether or not to prosecute is guided by a Code for Crown Prosecutors, which is publicly available. Crown prosecutors must first be satisfied that there is enough evidence to give rise to 'a realistic prospect of conviction'. They must take into account any likely defences. 'A realistic prospect of conviction' is defined as meaning that 'a jury or bench of magistrates, properly directed in accordance with the law, is more likely than not to convict the defendant of the charge alleged'. The Crown prosecutor must consider the evidence both admissible and reliable.

If the evidence passes the test, the Crown prosecutor must next apply the 'public interest' test. In 1951, the then Attorney General said in the House of Commons that, 'It has never been the rule in this country — and I hope it never will be — that suspected criminal offences must automatically be the subject of prosecution'; this remains the view to this day, and prosecutions are not brought unless it is in the public interest to do so. The Code for Crown Prosecutors lists a number of factors which would favour proceeding with a prosecution, for example:

— conviction is likely to result in a significant sentence;
— a weapon was used or violence threatened when the offence was committed;
— the victim was a person serving the public, such as a police officer or nurse;
— the defendant was in a position of trust;
— the victim was vulnerable and was put in considerable fear, or suffered some kind of personal attack;
— the offence was motivated by some form of discrimination.

On the other hand, certain other features may be persuasive that it is not in the public interest to prosecute; for instance, where:

— the offence was committed as a result of a genuine mistake or misunderstanding;
— prosecution is likely adversely to affect the victim's physical or mental health;
— the defendant is elderly or suffers from significant mental or physical ill health (although this factor alone is unlikely to be conclusive);
— if a prosecution went ahead, details which could harm sources of information, international relations or national security, might be made public.

If the CPS decides to proceed with a prosecution, a CPS lawyer will present the case in the magistrates' court, but usually instructs counsel to deal with cases that go to the Crown Court.

The CPS has obligations to observe confidentiality to protect witnesses, victims, suspects and defendants.

Despite the introduction of the CPS, criminal cases are still in theory brought in the name of the Crown, and, as we have noted, a case against a defendant with the surname Smith is called *'The Queen* v *Smith'*, or *'R* v *Smith'*.

The probation service

The probation service in each probation area is administered by a probation committee, comprising magistrates and others having appropriate knowledge and experience. The day-to-day management of the service is the responsibility of the Chief Probation Officer for the area. The probation committee employs the probation service staff, although they are paid by the local authority. It also sets policy for the running of the service.

In an area which is not a 'self-contained' probation area, i.e., where the same probation area covers more than one court area, each court area also has a probation liaison committee, consisting of a certain number of magistrates. Its purpose is to foster links between the magistrates and the probation service, making sure the magistrates are aware of the facilities provided by the probation service, and to give probation officers whatever help it can.

There are statutory rules governing appointment to the committees, term of office, meetings and officers. The work of the probation committee includes:

— appointing probation officers and ensuring that they carry out their work efficiently. Certain people, including magistrates, are disqualified from appointment as probation officers;

— assigning a probation officer to the Crown Court to which defendants may be committed for trial or sentence;

— assigning a probation officer as a welfare officer to the High Court and the county court to prepare reports in matrimonial cases;

— assigning a probation officer to prisons;

— providing the necessary accommodation and equipment for the service;

— maintaining records for at least five years concerning persons with whom the service has dealt;

— making arrangements for work under community service orders to be performed and appointing a community service committee to supervise the arrangements. The probation committee appoints the community service staff and makes arrangements for its premises and other facilities;

— providing and running bail hostels, probation hostels and other establishments.

The work of probation officers includes:

— supervising persons subject to probation orders, supervision orders or suspended sentence supervision orders, and 'advising, assisting and befriending' such persons;

— supervising persons subject to money payment supervision orders;

— preparing pre-sentence reports with a view to assisting the court in deciding on the most appropriate penalty;

— supervising persons released from prison and subject to supervision; and 'advising, assisting and befriending' prisoners during the twelve months after their release if they so wish;

— supervising persons discharged from hospital under the Mental Health Act who are subject to supervision;

— 'advising, assisting and befriending' those on bail who wish to be so helped;

— carrying out duties in connection with adoption, custody, reconciliation, consent to marriage, wards of courts and disputes concerning the welfare of children;
— making reports on the above activities and keeping records.

'National standards' for the probation service were introduced in 1995, setting down requirements to ensure consistency and high standards in all aspects of the service's work.

Her Majesty's Inspectorate of Probation, a division of the Home Office, has the task of inspecting and reporting on probation services with a view to ensuring that tasks are carried out properly and efficiently and promoting good standards of management and service.

The magistrates' courts committee

While the chairman of the bench and the clerk to the justices have overall responsibilities for the quality of justice dispensed in their courts, the task of organising and managing the courts falls to the magistrates' courts committee and the justices' chief executive. In accordance with the principle of the separation of powers, i.e., that judicial and administrative functions should be kept apart from each other to avoid the possibility that justice might be compromised by factors which are not directly relevant, the trend is towards allocating the judicial functions and administrative functions to separate persons or bodies, although, as has been mentioned, in some areas the justices' clerk is also the justices' chief executive.

Each area has a magistrates' court committee composed of magistrates for the area, who are elected in accordance with a procedure set out in statutory rules. One or two other members, who need not be magistrates, may be co-opted by the committee with the approval of the Lord Chancellor, or appointed by the Lord Chancellor. According to the Police and Magistrates' Courts Act 1994, the magistrates' courts committee is responsible 'for the efficient and effective administration of the magistrates' courts for their area'. The committee also appoints the justices' chief executive, subject to the Lord Chancellor's approval; in particular, the Lord Chancellor must approve the appointment of the same person as both justices' chief executive and clerk to the justices. The justices' chief executive is responsible for the day-to-day running of the court subject to the instructions of the committee. It has already been noted that, to preserve the independence of the clerk to the justices when advising magistrates, the clerk is not subject to any direction of the magistrates' court committee or the justices' chief executive.

The 1994 Act also legislated for openness in the work of the committee, requiring that at least one meeting a year is to be open to the public, and that the minutes of the committee meetings are to be open to inspection by the public except to the extent that they contain confidential information. Further, the Act allows the Lord Chancellor to require committees to keep magistrates informed of the committee's activities and to ascertain the views of magistrates on certain matters.

There is a view that it is an anachronism that committees of magistrates continue to be responsible for the administrative arrangements of the court, since the qualities by reference to which people are appointed as magistrates do not necessarily qualify them to run the administration. It is said in some quarters that the time has come for magistrates to confine themselves to their judicial duties and for the management of the courts to be transferred to professional appointees.

Her Majesty's Magistrates' Courts Service Inspectorate

A recent innovation is Her Majesty's Magistrates' Courts Service Inspectorate. This 'independent' body operates within the Lord Chancellor's Department and has a small staff charged with the duty of inspecting and reporting to the Lord Chancellor on the management and organisation of the magistrates' courts. The inspectors have no role in respect of judicial matters; they may not be present when a court is hearing proceedings in private or when magistrates are deliberating in the retiring room. But they do have powers of entry to the court house and have access to the records of the magistrates' courts committee and any other documents containing information about the administration of the courts.

Inspections consist of considering written material provided by magistrates' courts committees, discussions with managers, staff, court users and magistrates, and information gleaned from visiting courts, with a view to assessing the quality of service, the organisation of court work and the management of resources. On the basis of this information, and taking into account the characteristics of the area in question, the Inspectorate reports to the Lord Chancellor and may make recommendations for improvement to the relevant magistrates' courts committees.

The first reports were produced in 1994, and continue apace as the Inspectorate spreads its web across the country. Published responses by magistrates' courts committees are generally positive, welcoming an objective view and suggestions for improvement.

Other committees

Many benches also elect a number of other committees and panels with specific tasks. These may include:

— a penalties committee, which makes suggestions for 'starting point' penalties to supplement or vary those provided by the Magistrates' Association. For example, in an area where prostitution is a particular problem, the bench may wish to have some guidance on the starting point, this offence not being included in the Association's Guidelines. Or if there has been an outbreak of 'joy-riding', the bench may seek to deter it by adopting an entry point higher than suggested by the Association;

— a bench chairmanship committee, to implement chairmanship training and assess the results;

— the youth court panel. Magistrates sitting in the youth court need special aptitudes and training to deal with the different approach taken when dealing with the young; see Chapter 7;

— the family court panel: again membership of this panel requires special training; see Chapter 7;

— the licensing committee, which deals with liquor licensing in the area. Again, this calls for an understanding of a fairly complex set of rules; see Chapter 7.

In addition, the magistrates' courts committee may establish a training subcommittee, to make the necessary arrangements to ensure that all members of the bench receive at the least the minimum required training (see page 42).

The police

At one time, the magistrates' courts were commonly referred to as 'police courts', but this expression disappeared following a change in the law in 1948. The privatisation of court security and the prison escort service has further reduced the number of police officers regularly present in the courts.

It is widely accepted that one of the strengths of the police service is that it operates independently of central or local government. This accords with the general principle of the separation of powers — that the police, the judiciary and government bodies should each approach their work free of influence from each other. There are 43 police areas in

England and Wales, the areas being roughly equivalent to administrative counties.

The principal functions of the police are to keep law and order; protect people and property; prevent crime; detect criminals; liaise with the Crown Prosecution Service and control traffic. Volumes could be, and have been, written about what these duties entail. Only a few general principles are noted here. Thus, the police are subject to the law in the same way as everybody else; they may not bend it or break it, but they do have special powers, notably powers to detain, arrest, search and question people. These are limited by, for example, the Codes of Practice under the Police and Criminal Evidence Act 1984 ('PACE') which regulate police powers to stop and search people, to search premises and seize property and to detain and question people; identification procedures, including identification parades; and the tape recording of interviews. It has been said that 'The Codes of Practice are to protect the individual from the might of the state. An individual is at a great disadvantage when arrested by the police even when there is no impropriety'.

Police officers regularly appear as witnesses in the criminal courts. They have no special status as witnesses and there is no presumption that what they say is more likely to be true than what anybody else says. Lady Ralphs and Geoffrey Norman, in their book, *The Magistrate as Chairman*, refer to a 1974 case, where a conviction was overturned on appeal, because the chairman of the magistrates had made the wholly unacceptable statement that:

Quite the most unpleasant cases that we have to decide are those where the evidence is a direct conflict between a police officer and a member of the public. My principle in such cases has always been to believe the evidence of the police officer, and therefore we find the case proved.

On the other hand, the police are trained to observe people, events and surroundings accurately, and to make reliable notes, and magistrates will have this in mind when deciding what credibility and weight to assign to their evidence. But police officers are not immune from making genuine errors or misconstruing events. Even worse, in recent years there has been a number of notorious cases of wrongful convictions based on bad faith or malpractice by police officers. It remains rare for cases of this kind to come to light, but magistrates will be conscious of the possibility, however remote.

Training

Although there is no substitute for experience, training is nevertheless increasingly necessary. Preparatory training before new magistrates begin to sit has already been mentioned in Chapter 1. Further basic training is undertaken during the three years following appointment, four hours' training being required in both the second and third years. Basic training is usually provided at the magistrate's 'home' court. Those appointed since 1980, and chairmen, must also undertake twelve hours' training over each period of three years. Up to six hours of this training may be at the 'home' court, and the rest is 'away' — at county, regional or national level. Thus, the training officers for a number of courts — for a whole county, say — may pool their resources and skills to provide courses for all the magistrates in the county. Training is also provided by the Judicial Studies Board, the Magistrates' Association, the Lord Chancellor's Department, the University of Cambridge Extra-Mural Department and other organisations.

Unsurprisingly, the quality of training varies, but from the magistrate's point of view, it is gradually becoming more interesting and informative as techniques such as participation, role-playing, and the use of sample cases increasingly supplement the traditional lecture.

Training covers the entire ambit of the magistrate's work — from basic principles about how the system works, the standard of proof and the significance of the judicial oath and so on, through sentencing exercises, the principles of structured decision-making and how to enforce fines, to courses on how to train magistrates! Those appointed to the youth panel and the family panel undertake training specific to those special roles. In recent years, there has been such a plethora of new legislation that training courses have had to be devised to explain it all to the magistrates. Training may also take the form of presentations of the work of other agencies — the probation service, the police domestic violence unit and the community service organisation, for example.

After a few years experience on the bench, most magistrates are asked if they wish to undertake training for chairmanship. Most benches have a Bench Chairmanship Committee, elected by the members, which decides who will be invited. By the time such an invitation arrives, most magistrates, from their observation of chairmen at work, will have formed some views about which styles of chairmanship they admire and which they would prefer to avoid.

The purpose of training for chairmanship is to ensure that prospective chairmen, as well as having all the skills and virtues of a non-chairman magistrate, will be able to uphold the dignity and neutrality of the proceedings; deal with an unexpected turn of events; discern the material points of an argument; control his or her emotions and those of others; lead (but not dominate) discussions in the retiring room; and announce the decisions of the bench in a plain, straightforward way. All these must be done in full co-operation with magisterial colleagues, and without pomposity, self-importance or condescension. The Judicial Studies Board has said that training should cover, among other matters:

> speaking in court and, in particular, announcing decisions; handling various types of frequently occurring court-room situations; the relationship between the chairman and the wingers; the relationship between the chairman and the clerk; the role of the chairman in the retiring room.

These qualities may have already been developed in those who, in other contexts, have chaired meetings and discussions, but magistrates who have not had this kind of experience should not be put off — they may turn out to be better chairmen!

Training for chairmanship can sometimes be nerve-racking, as where the candidate chairman is asked to chair a mock trial, with a real-life Crown Prosecutor and defence solicitor both of whom regularly appear in the court proper; the clerk to the justices in the dock accused of stealing the petty cash to fund an addiction to liquorice allsorts; and a rabble of unruly magistrates in the public gallery!

There are many other sources of information about what distinguishes a good chairman from a bad one, not least the training itself, and little more need be said here, other than to highlight a few principles which may find favour: that a few moments thought-gathering silence are preferable to a garbled statement or calling the defendant by the wrong name; fewer words are almost always preferable to more; colleagues are to be consulted always, even if you are making the same decision for the eleventh time that morning and you know what their answers will be; police men and women can all be safely addressed as 'officer' to avoid inadvertently demoting them; if in any doubt, consult the legal advisor and/or ask colleagues to agree to retire; and last, what is said should be framed carefully and simply — if it were reported verbatim in the local newspaper, would it cause the chairman satisfaction or embarrassment?

Having completed the initial 'out of court' stage of chairmanship training, each trainee is assessed by the bench chairmanship committee, on the basis of the recommendations of experienced magistrates who have observed him or her in training, to decide whether or not they should proceed to the next phase. If so, the fledgling chairman takes the chair under the supervision of an experienced chairman and with an experienced legal advisor. Further appraisal takes place during, usually, six such sittings, and if all is well, the new chairman is then 'qualified'.

But that is not quite the end of the matter, for chairmen now undertake refresher training within six years of the basic chairmanship course, and thereafter further refresher training within six years of each earlier refresher course.

The chairman and deputy chairmen of the bench

Apart from chairmen of the courts, each bench has its bench chairman and deputy chairmen. Statutory rules establish the procedure for electing the chairman and deputies each year, by secret ballot, at the bench annual general meeting held in October. A procedure to identify a short list of candidates in advance of the election is often adopted. A chairman may hold office for not more than five consecutive years, although in many areas this is in practice reduced to three or four.

The task of the chairman of the bench is to act as leader and mentor. He or she needs to maintain and promote good working relationships with the justices' clerk, the justices' chief executive and the court staff, and with a variety of outside agencies; promote and participate in training; represent the bench at a variety of outside fora; and generally keep up to date with developments. In this work the chairman is aided by a number of elected deputy chairmen. Often individual magistrates are assigned to a particular deputy chairman to whom they can turn for guidance in their work as a magistrate. The outlook of the chairman and deputies tends to rub off on the bench as a whole, so that, generally, a positive, constructive and supportive approach is conducive to a harmonious, well-trained and efficient bench of magistrates.

The role of the chairman of the bench does not itself extend to administrative or organisational matters, although the chairman of the bench may also be a member of the magistrates' court committee.

The view that persons may be particularly eligible for election as chairman by reason of length of service alone is falling into disfavour. Experience matters, of course, but the trend is towards emphasising the search for the qualities of leadership which go to make an effective chairman.

Newer members of a bench may have difficulty in deciding who is to have their vote for chairman, since they may not know the candidates well, or even at all. The extent of canvassing or distribution of information about the candidates varies from place to place, some magistrates apparently taking the view that such activities are unseemly, others seeing no reason to outlaw these elements of a democratic process.

The timetable

Each court has a system for timetabling, registering and recording the number of times magistrates attend. How often a magistrate sits in court clearly depends on how many magistrates there are on the bench; how many cases are being brought; and the number of court rooms and other facilities available. It has already been mentioned in Chapter 1 that the usual minimum is 26 half-day sittings a year, but in busy areas magistrates may sit twice as often as this. At the other end of the scale, lay magistrates are supposed to be just that — lay, not professional, justices. For this reason, they should not sit so often that they verge on becoming professional, and disproportionately high numbers of sittings are generally discouraged.

How sittings are planned varies from place to place. In some areas, individual justices are allocated to a particular day of the week, and so may be 'Monday justices', 'Tuesday justices' and so on. This type of arrangement is sometimes said to have the weakness that the practices of the justices of a particular day may become entrenched, with the result that, say, the 'Tuesday justices' may be considered more lenient, or more severe, than the 'Wednesday justices'. In an extreme case, this may lead parties to seek to have matters listed on a particular day because they perceive that as conducive to the result they desire. This system also restricts the opportunities justices have to meet each other and exchange views and ideas.

Another system features advance allocation at random (although, as is noted below, there are many considerations which restrict how 'random' the process can in fact be), so that justices constantly sit with different colleagues. This meets the two criticisms of the 'day' system mentioned above. Rotas devised in this way may be compiled quarterly, half-yearly or annually, and justices may be given the opportunity to notify in advance dates or days on which they will not be able to sit.

Whichever system is adopted, those drawing up the lists have an unenviable task, for this is a clear example of 'you can't please all the people all the time'. These are just some of the factors that have to be taken into account when drawing up the rota:

— a balance between men and women;
— an appropriate mix of experience;
— sufficient qualified chairmen to take the courts of the day;
— if a family or youth court will be in session, the appropriate number of members of the youth panel or family panel will be needed;
— if chairmanship training is in progress, the courts will have to be arranged so that a trainee chairman sits with the allocated assessor;
— if an individual magistrate is coming back for the sentencing of an offender on whose trial that magistrate sat, that magistrate must be assigned to the appropriate court.

There are also varying arrangements for dealing with the situation where a magistrate is unable to sit on a date allocated, perhaps because of work commitments or because some emergency arises. In some courts, magistrates can simply arrange between themselves to exchange sessions; it is good practice to exchange with a colleague of the same sex and of roughly equal experience; and for qualified chairmen to exchange with other qualified chairmen, to maintain balance. In other courts, exchanges are channelled through a member of the court staff. 'Advertisements' seeking exchanges may appear on the retiring room notice board.

The custom of the court may be that all magistrates attending on a particular day are allocated in advance, by the rota clerk, to individual courts. Or they may be assigned to particular courts just before the session begins, by a senior magistrate who is 'chairman of the day'.

The rota can be a vexatious matter since it is often impossible to meet every magistrate's preferences — and people often do not know what their commitments will be at the time a rota is prepared. Again, different people have different views about priorities; if a particular date is difficult, some will seek to change the court date; others will seek to change the other, conflicting engagement. Flexibility on the part of magistrates will always be appreciated, but sometimes work or family must be the primary consideration. If a magistrate cannot attend at the last minute because of illness or some sudden emergency, the simple courtesy of a telephone call is of course essential.

It is possible that two magistrates assigned to the same court do not get along with each other particularly well. By and large, this is probably just too bad and they have to get on with it — broad-mindedness is an attribute of a good magistrate, and life would be tedious indeed if we were all the same. But there may come a point when it is wise for the individuals concerned to question where the difficulty lies. If a magistrate has a real and continuing problem working alongside another individual, particularly perhaps if he or she perceives that the other person exercises certain preconceptions, then it may well be a matter on which the allocated deputy chairman or chairman of the bench should be consulted.

Four

Jurisdiction

Introduction

The range of work undertaken in magistrates' courts, and the extent of those courts' powers, are extremely wide. Magistrates' courts have both temporal and geographical jurisdiction. However, there are limitations on their powers, whether they be limitations on trial powers or powers of sentence. Subordinate legislation contains powers to delegate certain of the functions of magistrates' courts to others.

Magistrates, as distinct from the courts in which they sit, have limited jurisdiction in that each is appointed to a particular commission area and has no powers outside that commission area, and they themselves have temporal jurisdiction in that they are obliged to retire from the bench at the age of 70, with the exception of the chairman of the bench, who is obliged to retire at the end of the year in which he or she reaches the age of 70.

Magistrates' courts are often expressed to be 'creatures of statute' but many who use that phrase have no precise idea of what it means. In fact it means that the courts themselves are governed by statute law. Any powers they have are strictly constrained and defined by statute. By contrast, for example, the High Court has various non-statutory powers, such as the power to deal with contempt, and a power to secure the protection of children by use of wardship as part of its residuary power to safeguard the welfare of the young. It must be said that the general trend is for residuary powers to become progressively less important as statute law becomes progressively more comprehensive, although it is sometimes helpful for the High Court to use its residuary jurisdiction to fill gaps that even the Parliamentary draftsman has not considered. All powers that magistrates' courts have to deal with children, however, are to be found in the body of a statute: there is no residuary power.

This does not mean that other sources of law do not fall to be considered in the magistrates' courts. Several offences, such as murder, manslaughter, and certain conspiracies are contrary to common law and all must be tried at the Crown Court, but there are certain common law powers exercisable by magistrates, such as the centuries-old power to bind a person over to keep the peace and/or be of good behaviour. Legal purists do not like these powers which are often incapable of precise definition, and the Law Commission has recommended abolition of the common law power to bind over.

A close parallel to the framework of magistrates' courts is that of the county courts, the civil court of first instance. That too is a creature of statute deriving its powers from a succession of County Court Acts, starting in the mid nineteenth century, and being supplemented by a vast body of rules under which the jurisdiction of those courts operates.

Magistrates: appointment and jurisdiction

One of the most important characteristics of the magistracy that can be traced down through the centuries is the concept of a locally based institution discharging its duties in local areas. This was so as long ago as the twelfth century when magistrates had something of a peacekeeping role. Whether it will continue to be as much a feature in the future one cannot say. There is no groundswell of opinion seeking to change the local base, although nowadays, with vastly improved communications, when all parts of the country can be kept abreast with trends in crime, trends in society and other developments, it is at least arguable that local approaches and local attitudes should be of lesser importance. Indeed there is some suggestion that the approach to sentencing offenders should be the same whether the offence is committed in Berwick-upon-Tweed or in Penzance. If a man pleads guilty to assaulting his wife, causing injury, should there be any difference in approach if the offence is committed in Carlisle rather than in London? That, however, looks more to the manner in which magistrates' powers should be exercised than to the manner of appointment. There is something to be said for an enthusiastic and well trained lay magistracy which is appointed from, and broadly representative of, the community which it seeks to serve. Justice at the lowest level can be more sensitively and efficiently delivered from local roots.

As we have seen in Chapter 1, the Lord Chancellor is responsible for the appointment of the 30,000 justices for England and Wales. Each is appointed to a particular commission area which is normally co-terminous with an administrative county, under the *custos rotulorum* ('keeper of the rolls') who is the Lord Lieutenant for the county concerned. Greater London has its own arrangements, which differ somewhat from the rest of the country, and Outer London is divided into four commission areas: Middlesex, North East London, South East London, and South West London. The Lord Chancellor does not vet every nomination to the magistracy personally, although it is said that Lord Hailsham used to insist on reading each of the nomination forms.

It has also been noted in Chapter 1 that the Lord Chancellor appoints an advisory committee for each commission area which is charged with recommending to him people who are thought suitable for appointment. Advisory committee members may be appointed for between three and twelve years, and include magistrates and non-magistrates. Until comparatively recently, the names of members were not publicised, presumably to prevent canvassing, but that has now changed. The advisory committee will have to assess the strength of each bench in its area. This may include data about workload and whether it is rising or falling, the number of magistrates retiring or resigning, and any particular features, such as likely changes to the composition of the bench or the area within the next few years. Comments will be invited from those who can assist with this information, such as chairmen of benches and clerks to the justices. A picture will be built up of how many candidates will need to be recommended in any current cycle.

The appointment will be to the commission area, and the new magistrate is usually sworn in before the Crown Court liaison judge. The new magistrate is assigned to a petty sessional division ('area' in London and the former Metropolitan counties). The petty sessional division is an administrative area, so that a magistrate appointed to the commission of Blankshire may be appointed to the Greentown petty sessional division. The magistrate's legal authority is for the county of Blankshire, however, and he or she can therefore lawfully sit as a magistrate in any court in Blankshire.

Apart from swearing in new magistrates, the liaison judge may perform a number of important roles with regard to the magistracy. He may be a co-opted member of the magistrates' courts committee which is charged with employing the staff in justices' clerks' offices, overseeing the management of court buildings, and the organisation and delivery of training. He may also be a member of the Probation Committee, which fulfils broadly similar functions with regard to the probation service. More importantly, he can be regarded as a 'guide, philosopher and friend' of all magistrates. No doubt a magistrate with a particular worry or concern would normally turn to the chairman of the bench, or the justices' clerk, but common concerns can sometimes be assuaged by the advice of someone not involved in the day-to-day operation of the magistrates' courts. Occasionally the liaison judge may wish to talk to the magistrates about sentencing, the important bail or custody decision, mode of trial, or a range of other issues of importance.

The magistrate in the Crown Court

Magistrates do not sit merely in magistrates' courts. After a couple of years on the bench, they will be entitled to sit in the Crown Court hearing appeals and committals for sentence (although obviously not in respect of cases they have heard below). They sit with a judge or a recorder and they have an equal vote with the judge, but are expected to follow the judge's guidance on the law. Magistrates should take any opportunity that presents itself to sit in the Crown Court. They will find invaluable the experience of hearing cases when sitting with a judge.

Retirement

It has been noted that the general rule is that a magistrate must retire no later than his or her 70th birthday. Magistrates are, however, permitted to continue to sit as justices of the Crown Court for a further two years, until their 72nd birthdays. The reason for this difference is presumably to bring justices in the Crown Court up to the same age limit as circuit judges, but it is something of an anomaly that for those two years a magistrate, deprived of the right to sit in the magistrates' 'natural habitat', can sit in the Crown Court.

When a magistrate retires he or she can apply to be transferred to the supplemental list. This list is maintained by the Clerk of the Crown in Chancery, and the names of retiring magistrates may be placed on it as some recognition of their years of service. A magistrate on the supplemental list has certain powers, although these obviously do not include sitting in a court in a judicial capacity, save for the Crown Court exemption noted above. After a magistrate's name has been placed on the list, he or she may:

— sign any document for the purpose of authenticating another person's signature;

— take and authenticate by his or her signature any written declaration not made on oath; and

— give a certificate of facts within his or her knowledge or of his or her opinion as to any matter.

Despite the apparent breadth of the last item listed above, the status of a supplemental list magistrate is largely honorific, except in one respect. We have seen that magistrates are appointed to particular commission areas. If a magistrate moves out of the area, for example on a change of job, he or she becomes residentially disqualified. In view of the experience gained, it would be a serious waste if the individual had to be nominated to be a magistrate and go through the selection procedures all over again. What is likely to happen is that the magistrate will apply to be placed on the supplemental list, and then when a vacancy occurs in the area to which the magistrate has moved, he or she may be 'reactivated' and appointed for that commission area. If the gap in time is other than very short, the Lord Chancellor may require the magistrate to undertake some refresher training to become acquainted with developments in the law and sentencing since he or she was placed on the supplemental list.

The statutory framework of magistrates' courts

The main statute governing the work of the magistrates' courts is the Magistrates' Courts Act 1980, which brings together a number of former measures into one Act. The principal Act before then was the Magistrates' Courts Act 1952, but various later measures were incorporated, for example the provisions of the Magistrates' Courts Act 1957, which introduced the procedure providing for guilty pleas in absence, which is considered in greater detail in Chapter 6. The 1980 Act is certainly not a codifying measure, because much material governing the work of these courts is to be found elsewhere — see, for example, the provisions of the Criminal Justice Acts 1967–1991, and the Police and Criminal Evidence Act 1984.

The 1980 Act, although not comprehensive, is the first base for anyone considering the powers of these courts. It deals with a number of important aspects of the law. Part I deals with the criminal jurisdiction and procedure of the court and contains 50 sections which cope with everyday procedures followed by all magistrates' courts in England and Wales. Part II deals with civil jurisdiction and procedure. It is easy to categorise magistrates' courts as criminal courts of summary jurisdiction only. In fact, they retain a substantial civil jurisdiction, most obviously, though not exclusively, in the field of family law. These sections in the Act start from the commencement of civil proceedings by the issue of a complaint (or application) through to the enforcement of a civil debt, and the imposition of penalties for non-compliance with non-monetary orders of the court in this jurisdiction. Part III deals with satisfaction and enforcement generally; Part IV with witnesses and evidence; Part V with appeals from the magistrates' courts whether to the Crown Court or by case stated to the High Court; Part VI with recognisances (i.e., solemn obligations or promises backed by a sum of money) and Part VII with miscellaneous and supplementary matters. There are in addition a number of schedules dealing in more detail with particular aspects of the jurisdiction.

For legal advisors, the 1980 Act is a familiar, accessible source of the law used day in, day out. It is the first Act that a trainee lawyer in the courts will have to master. For the new magistrate, it is perhaps not worth studying as a text, but many of the provisions will become familiar. As explained above, the 1980 Act is not the full story, but it is often the reference point for both lawyer and magistrate. Other Acts and case law decisions often need to be interpreted against its provisions. A host of other Acts, some of which are considered elsewhere in this handbook, deal with specific topics, such as evidence or costs, which might be of particular importance at different times depending on the issues arising during a sitting. The Magistrates' Courts Act 1980 is *always* important.

Subordinate legislation affecting jurisdiction

Even an important Act can only provide a framework. It can provide the power of the court in certain circumstances to issue a witness summons, or to rectify an earlier mistake. But any Act, however comprehensive, cannot go into the nuts and bolts of how the power may be applied. For that, one usually looks to subordinate legislation which has been mentioned earlier. It is worth considering for a moment how important that can be.

The Magistrates' Courts Act 1980 has as its subordinate legislation the Magistrates' Courts Rules 1981 in which much of the detailed mechanism for the working of the Act is prescribed. The rules are made under the authority of the Act. We saw that the Act dealt, in Part V, with appeals from the magistrates' courts. The rules prescribe what a notice of appeal must contain, what the court must do when it receives an appeal, what documents have to be forwarded to the appellate court, and the timescale in which that must be done. In other words, a simple and straightforward provision in the Act has to be 'filled out' so that the appeal can be heard promptly and so that the appellate court has all requisite documents before it. The Act provides for how a summons may be applied for and issued; the rules provide the form which the summons must take, and the approved methods by which it may be served.

That is not the end of the story. Even these rules, and there are over 100 of them, can only impinge on the mechanics of magistrates' courts procedure, and statutes governing particular aspects of the jurisdiction often have their own subordinate legislation, to which the court may need to be referred. Thus, the Prosecution of Offences Act 1985 includes a Part dealing with costs in criminal cases, and details the powers that the court may have in given circumstances, but that tells only part of the story. The advocate or legal advisor researching a point may well need to consider, among other measures, the Costs in Criminal Cases (General) Regulations 1986 and the Costs in Criminal Cases (General) Regulations 1986 – Rates of Allowance, both of which were promulgated under powers contained in the 1985 Act. The Children Act 1989 provides a further example. That much heralded and comprehensive legislation has given rise to subordinate legislation to prescribe how it should work in certain circumstances: e.g., the Children (Admissibility of Hearsay Evidence) Order 1993, the Family Proceedings Courts (Children Act 1989) Rules 1991, the Children (Allocation of Proceedings) Order 1991, and others.

One of the most important pieces of subordinate legislation strikes a balance between the exercise of powers by the magistrates and by the justices' clerk. The 1980 Act refers to magistrates granting a summons, or committing for trial, but even before that Act certain judicial powers could be exercised by the justices' clerk. The Justices' Clerks Rules 1970, made under the Justices of the Peace Acts 1949–1968, specify a number of matters authorised to be done by a single justice of the peace for a petty sessions area, but which may be done 'by, to or before the justices' clerk for the area'. These include: the issue of a summons, including a witness summons; the committal for trial of a person on bail without consideration of the evidence, where that person has previously been on bail; the appointment of a guardian *ad litem* or solicitor for a child under s. 41, Children Act 1989; allowing further time for payment of a sum enforceable by a magistrates' court. As justices' clerks are often nowadays involved in matters of administration, is the delegation under the Rules capable of further delegation? The Rules themselves provide the answer. The powers may be exercisable by a justices' clerk's deputy or assistant provided that the individual concerned has been specifically authorised by the justices' clerk for that purpose, such authorisation being in writing.

The geographical and temporal jurisdiction of magistrates' courts

In an earlier section of this chapter we looked at the magistrate's own jurisdiction, namely that he or she is appointed to a commission area and fulfils duties within that area. But many of the matters the magistrate will deal with in court arise outside the commission area, and he or she may deal with them perfectly lawfully. For example, a magistrate may be asked to consider an application for a search warrant, to try to recover some illegally held drugs or firearms or stolen property. Such an application should always be checked by a member of the court staff to ensure that the magistrate has the necessary authority, but in some cases the application may be in respect of premises outside the commission area. There may be good reason for this. Perhaps it is part of a large enquiry which has been based in the commission area, and various search warrants are being sought, for premises within and outside the commission area; if the application is satisfactory in other respects, there is absolutely no reason why a warrant should not be granted to search premises outside the commission area.

It will be remembered that charges brought before the court can concern indictable, either way, and summary offences. For the purposes of geographical jurisdiction, either way offences can be considered as though they were indictable offences. These allegations can be charged at any criminal court in England and Wales, so that it is technically correct for, say, a murder that is alleged to have been committed in Swansea to be charged in London, and for theft of a bicycle in London to be charged in Sheffield. Serious allegations arising out of acts of terrorism may be charged in a court with a high level of security many miles away from the venue of the incident. It is a different story in the case of summary offences, which are generally the least serious and most numerous in the magistrates' court. Here the commission area assumes great importance, because these matters must normally be prosecuted at a court within the commission area where the offence is alleged to have taken place. Thus an offence of driving whilst disqualified alleged to have been committed in the Middlesex Commission Area of Greater London could not normally be charged at Sheffield. The exception to that sensible rule arises where the defendant already faces other summary matters at, in this example, Sheffield. Then it is possible to 'marry them up' so that one court can deal with all matters. This power should be contrasted with the power to remit to another court for sentence. That power arises only where a defendant has been convicted (either on plea or after evidence) at both courts and the receiving court consents. The summary offences at each court must carry either the power of imprisonment or the power to disqualify.

As with geographical jurisdiction, so with temporal jurisdiction. Indictable offences and either way offences can generally be prosecuted at any time, and there is no limit as to time. Summary offences generally have a time limit of six months in which the prosecutor may 'lay an information' (as to which, see pages 66–7), unless a statute allows a longer period (as does, for example, the social security legislation). This general rule must be qualified. There have been countless cases where prosecutions have been stopped because the High Court has felt that to proceed would constitute an abuse of the process of the court. There is an overriding need in the criminal justice system to ensure that the defendant has a fair trial, and a proper opportunity to dispute and defend the allegations made. Therefore the trial should take place as soon as is reasonably practicable and consistent with the need for both prosecution and defence to prepare their cases. It follows that if the prosecution were to seek to delay instituting proceedings so as to gain some unfair advantage, or if they did not follow normal procedures for the service of summonses, or any one of a number of things which caused delay, the defendant could apply to the High Court for judicial review, seeking an order of prohibition directing the justices not to hear the case. Even with the comparatively short time limit for a summary offence, there have been cases where *for no good reason* the prosecutor has delayed laying the information until just before the statutory time limit was about to expire and this has been held on the given facts to be an abuse of process and proceedings have been stayed (i.e., stopped). Conversely, there have been cases where there has been found to be no abuse of process where the trial has taken place years after the allegations complained of.

Examples of this are serious sexual offences and child abuse cases where the complaint has been made only after the allegedly abused child has attained adulthood.

Mode of trial and powers of sentence

The other type of jurisdiction that we need to consider involves the seriousness of an offence. Elsewhere in this book there is a detailed explanation of the mode of trial procedure (see page 68) under which a defendant may be offered trial at either the Crown Court or the magistrates' court. If the magistrates' court considers the matter too serious to be dealt with in that court, or the defendant, when offered summary trial, elects to be tried in the Crown Court, then he or she will be 'committed'. This means that the proceedings will be adjourned to a date, usually four to six weeks later, when, if it is shown that there is sufficient evidence to put the defendant on trial, the defendant will be sent to the Crown Court for trial. Committal proceedings are explained in greater detail in Chapter 5.

If, however, the defendant consents to being dealt with in the magistrates' court, then that court is constrained by the maximum penalties that the court may impose. The general limit for either way offences is a fine on level 5 (for an explanation of fine levels see Chapter 9) and/or a maximum term of imprisonment of six months. If there are two or more indictable offences, the maximum term of imprisonment is twelve months. The maximum for a summary offence is either a fine on level 5 and/or a maximum term of six months no matter how many summary offences there are, or the maximum for the offence, whichever is the less. Many summary offences carry a maximum less than the magistrates' courts' maximum, for example many summary offences do not carry any form of custodial penalty. The jurisdiction of the magistrates is strictly limited by these rules. In many courts the maxima are shown on the court lists handed to magistrates before going into court. If not, or if the information is unclear, the magistrate should always ask the legal advisor.

Out-of-court duties

Many courts have their own procedures for dealing with out-of-court applications and it is important that these are known. The magistrate who lives close to a busy police station or to a social services headquarters may be approached more often than is strictly necessary. Magistrates should always remember that although they should try to be helpful, the out-of-court application is to be avoided unless really necessary, and it is most important that if such an application has to be heard it should be heard judicially and with a certain formality.

How important or urgent is the application? If the application purports to be made directly by an applicant during normal office hours it will seldom be appropriate to consider it. The proper procedure for the applicant is to attend the justices' clerk's office and have the application checked. If a court is sitting, it is generally possible for the application to be fitted in between cases, or a case interrupted for the time it will take to have the application considered. Then it can be done in court, with the opportunity to consult the legal advisor about any legal implications, and with the ready availability of legal textbooks to check any point about which there may be doubt.

Sometimes, for example when a court does not sit daily, there may be no option other than to hear the application at the magistrate's home, but it is still a sensible policy for the magistrate to check whether the applicant has gone through the clerk's office. Indeed, you would normally expect the first point of contact to be by the clerk to the magistrate, explaining that there is to be an application and perhaps filling in some of the background, so that the magistrate can be confident, when hearing the application, that he or she knows precisely what must be established if the application is to be granted.

This leaves the comparatively rare situation where a magistrate is approached directly by the applicant, possibly late at night or at a weekend. A well regulated court will have distributed contact telephone numbers so that a magistrate can always obtain necessary advice, and prospective applicants may well have been circulated with the names and telephone numbers of more experienced magistrates who are familiar with applications of this kind. But however well run the organisation, there may always be instances when the less experienced magistrate may be approached, and it is impossible to get advice, either from a legal advisor or from a senior magistrate colleague. What should happen then?

The first point is that the magistrate should not panic. He or she should approach the matter with proper formality even if the application is being dealt with in the kitchen among a pile of dirty plates! It goes without saying that the applicant should be asked to produce identity before being allowed in. The magistrate should not make do with a cursory glance but should check the identity carefully. Next the magistrate should make sure the application is in written form; this will usually (although not always) mean that part of it will be on a pre-printed form. The gaps on the form must have been filled in before the magistrate starts, and the information must have been signed. The applicant must take an oath or affirmation that he or she is swearing to the truth of what he or she says. If a Bible or other appropriate holy book cannot be found, then the applicant, whether of any religion or none, can be asked to affirm. The precise wording is not crucial, but this is as good as any:

> I do solemnly sincerely and truly declare and affirm that this is my name and handwriting, and the contents of this my information are true to the best of my knowledge and belief.

The magistrate must read the information before the applicant is sworn, and then the applicant must be asked to explain the reason for the application in simple terms. The magistrate will then have received the information twice, and have had some opportunity to make a preliminary assessment of it. There may be questions which should be asked. If so, the magistrate must ask them and must always act judicially. An application must never be rubber stamped. The grant of a warrant will almost certainly affect the liberty or property of a fellow citizen, and should be made only if there appear to be good grounds to do so. Finally, and most importantly, a magistrate must never be pressurised into granting a warrant if not happy to do so. Applicants often give the impression of being rushed. They may be. They often give the impression that the application is very important and urgent. It may be. They may imply that it is a matter of life and death. It may be, but that is more doubtful.

Many applications could in fact wait until the next morning. But even if it is critical and a matter of life or death, the magistrate must take a step back and be prepared to reflect on the merits of the application. If the magistrate is not satisfied, then the application must be refused. Acting judicially requires no more than taking proper care in evaluating the merits of any application, and making a logical decision after the application has been made and, if necessary, clarified.

If an application is considered and a warrant granted and handed to the applicant, it is advisable for the magistrate to retain the information and send or deliver it as soon as is convenient to the justices' clerk's office. A telephone call the next working day to tell the clerk about the application will be appreciated, and will enable a record of the application to be made.

Stipendiary magistrates

In addition to the lay magistracy, there is also a stipendiary bench or, to be more accurate, two stipendiary benches: the metropolitan stipendiary magistrates and the provincial stipendiary magistrates. Although the provision for their appointment falls under different sections of the Justices of the Peace Act 1979, their powers are similar.

Basically, a stipendiary magistrate has all the powers of a bench of magistrates sitting in court, so it may be said that one stipendiary equals three lay magistrates. Stipendiaries are paid lawyers. They are usually appointed to busy urban areas. Metropolitan magistrates, over 60 in number, sit within the Inner London Commission Area in petty sessions, youth and family work. They normally sit with lay justices in youth and family work, although that is not obligatory. Provincial stipendiary magistrates sit in busy courts in the rest of the country. There are four stipendiaries in Birmingham, three in Liverpool, three in Manchester, two in Nottinghamshire, and one in county areas such as Essex, Norfolk, and Sussex. Many commission areas have not requested that a stipendiary be appointed, but generally if an advisory committee were to recommend such an appointment to the Lord Chancellor because of increasing workloads and/or insufficient suitable candidates for appointment to the lay bench, the Lord Chancellor would normally agree. The appointment is not within the Lord Chancellor's gift, but is made by the Queen on his recommendation.

Some lay magistrates, though happily only a few, consider the appointment of a stipendiary as the 'thin end of the wedge'. They express fears that a stipendiary magistrate will take all the interesting work leaving the more routine work to them. Others foresee an increase in the influence of professionals to the detriment of the enthusiastic, trained lay magistracy. Successive Lord Chancellors have sought to set these concerns at rest. Indeed it does not take a great aptitude in arithmetic to work out that there would not be adequate numbers of suitable lawyers to replace 30,000 lay magistrates, nor would the budgets be sufficient to pay for them. The most suitable solution is that all busy areas should have the use of one or more stipendiaries who can work alongside their lay colleagues in harmony, bringing their complementary skills to the pre-eminent task of doing justice in the area concerned. An authoritative working party report, published in 1996, made a series of recommendations, which will assist and enhance the smooth working relationship of the lay and stipendiary benches.

Five

Criminal Proceedings

Introduction

The aim of the criminal justice system must be, among other things, to ensure a fair system of trial and sentence for all those accused of crime; to ensure that those who are guilty either plead or are found guilty and then sentenced, and those who are innocent are acquitted; that these processes are completed without undue delay, and at acceptable cost. It can soon be seen that the work of the court is but one part of a larger system with a considerable degree of interdependence between the major players: the police, the CPS, the courts, the prison service, the probation service etc. On any view it is not a unified, but instead rather a disparate, system with every part of it having its own culture and priorities. But over the last 20 years there has been a great deal of recognition that mutual co-operation is the only way to make progress and this has been apparent with multi-agency meetings at national, regional and local level which have done much to break down barriers. In a real sense the court system finds itself at the fulcrum, and although there are important functions in the criminal justice system which do not involve the courts in any way (for example the process under which offenders are diverted from the courts when cautioned by the police), the vast majority of cases come into court for determination and conclusion.

How a case comes to court

A criminal case begins by way of charge, summons, or a warrant of first instance. In non-criminal proceedings the usual procedure is by application or complaint, but those methods are not considered in this chapter. If a police officer has reasonable cause to suspect that there is evidence to justify proceedings against an individual, that individual may be arrested *without warrant* if the offence is an 'arrestable offence'. An arrestable offence is one that carries five or more years' imprisonment on indictment. But there is a whole range of offences which do not fall within the definition of arrestable offences and yet carry the power of arrest — driving whilst disqualified and driving a motor vehicle whilst unfit through drink or drugs are both good examples. Here statute provides the power of arrest. In addition such a power exists in respect of conduct which may not even be criminal, such as the power to arrest for a breach of the peace. A person so arrested will be brought before the court by way of a civil complaint for breach of the peace which, if proved or admitted, will result in an order binding the defendant over in a sum of money for a period of time. The law relating to the arrest of suspects without warrant is now to be found in Part III of the Police and Criminal Evidence Act 1984 (PACE).

In addition, there are wide powers for the police to arrest suspects *with* a warrant; for example where only a description of the offender is known at first, but evidence of the identity of the suspect is obtained later, or where a police officer is enforcing the attendance of a defendant before the courts. An information (brief details of the conduct complained of) must have been laid before the court and some evidence on oath or affirmation given to substantiate the information before the court will in its discretion consider issuing a warrant. The grant of a warrant is a judicial act, and the court must never 'rubber stamp' the issue of a warrant. Indeed the court should ask pertinent questions to try to ascertain whether there are reasonable grounds for the issue of a warrant.

Whether the power of arrest is exercisable with or without warrant, from the moment of arrest, the procedure which the police are obliged to follow will be the same.

Certainly from the moment of arrest and in some cases beforehand — for example where the police have searched the suspect or the suspect's property — there are very strict provisions governing police conduct. Some of these are statutory and some are non-statutory but operate within a statutory framework. The most important are the Codes of Practice made under PACE which specify how the police (and other investigatory bodies, such as HM Customs & Excise) should conduct themselves in given situations. The Codes of Practice are considered in more detail below.

When an arrest is effected

The first requirement for the police on arresting a suspect is to tell the suspect the reason for the arrest, unless it is impracticable to do so. Plainly if the police intervene to restore order in a disturbance and the suspect violently resists detention, it may not be practicable to explain the reason until later, although the reason may be obvious. The police are then required to take the suspect to a police station where he will be put before the custody officer, normally a police sergeant, who is completely independent of the investigation and whose duties are to protect suspects in detention and take steps to safeguard his welfare. That duty is a positive one and all dealings with a detainee must be recorded in writing in a document known as the 'custody record'. Thus routine checks on well-being, the times refreshment is given, and the occasions of removal from the cells for any reason all have to be noted in the record.

Time limits

There are very strict limits on the time a detainee may be held in custody without charge. The police are required to charge as soon as they have evidence which in their judgment would sustain a case. Some evidence may be obtained after arrest, such as the detainee's answers to questions in interview conducted at the police station, but it would be manifestly unfair to hold a detainee endlessly whilst evidence is amassed in dribs and drabs. The police will have some evidence against a detainee before arrest, but as the arrest is an infringement of liberty, PACE states that time in custody before charge should be limited. The limit is usually 24 hours, but that may be extended in the case of a serious arrestable offence (as defined in the Act) by a further 12 hours ('continued detention') on the authority of an officer not below the rank of superintendent. Strict criteria must be fulfilled before this power is exercisable. If the police are still not in a position to charge when the additional 12 hours have expired, they may apply to a magistrates' court for a warrant of further detention when similar criteria will apply. In brief the court must be satisfied that:

— the suspect's detention without charge is necessary to secure/ preserve evidence;
— the offence is a serious arrestable offence;
— the investigation is being conducted diligently and expeditiously.

Such an application is heard by magistrates in a closed courtroom, but with the suspect and the suspect's lawyer present. The suspect or the suspect's lawyer may challenge the grounds on which it is sought to extend the period of detention. The magistrates, provided they are satisfied that the statutory criteria are made out, may extend the period for up to 36 hours, and there may be a further application for an extension to the warrant of further detention, subject to an absolute maximum of 96 hours. The vast majority of enquiries are over well within that period, and applications for warrants of further detention remain comparatively rare. Indeed in the broad spectrum of cases with which the police have to deal, charges are preferred after just a few hours — a lengthy detention before charge is a relative rarity. It goes without saying that if the police do not have enough evidence to charge and the investigation is effectively at an end, they must release the detainee forthwith.

The charging process

If there is enough evidence to justify the detainee being charged, the detainee is taken before the charging officer, who is an officer at the police station, and the charge or charges will be read over. The detainee will have been cautioned on arrest and again before any interview that may have taken place. The detainee is cautioned again, and asked if he or she wishes to say anything in answer to the charge. The charge or charges will have been written on a self-carbonating form known as the charge sheet, before being read out. A copy of the form is handed to the detainee.

Bail granted or refused?

At the same time, the police make a decision as to whether the defendant is to be bailed to court, with or without conditions, or whether bail should be denied, in which case the defendant must be taken to the magistrates' court as soon as is practicable. This means in any event within 24 hours, excluding Sundays, Christmas Day, and Good Friday. The decision as to whether bail should be granted at that time is wholly that of the police. PACE lays down the considerations that apply. The defendant may be a person whose name and address cannot be ascertained or verified. There may be reasonable grounds for believing that the defendant would commit an offence or offences if bailed. The circumstances of the instant allegation and previous criminal convictions (if any) may provide some guidance. Are there reasonable grounds for believing the defendant would interfere with witnesses or otherwise obstruct justice? Should the defendant be kept in custody for his or her own protection? Would the imposition of bail and conditions meet those fears?

If the police are of the opinion that the defendant can be safely bailed, they grant bail and the defendant signs a part of the charge sheet acknowledging the duty to surrender to the custody of a specified magistrates' court at a specified date/time. If not bailed, the defendant will be brought before the next sitting of the magistrates' court and the magistrates will decide whether or not to grant bail, applying the criteria referred to in Chapter 8. With the charge sheet, the defendant will be given other documents, explaining how to make an application for legal aid. Many defendants are advised at the police station by a duty solicitor, who will already have explained the defendant's rights to him or her.

Between charge and court

Practice varies in different parts of the country, but there are usually several weeks between the time the defendant is charged at the police station and the first appearance at court. There is some debate as to whether or not that delay is a good thing. It was once the case that defendants would be bailed to a court sitting the next morning or a couple of days later at most. Nowadays the weeks are meant to be put to good use by both prosecution and defence. The police have to prepare a prosecution file against the defendant and send it to the CPS, so that their review procedure can be undertaken. The charge and the available evidence will be scrutinised by a Crown Prosecutor to decide whether there is enough evidence to sustain a reasonable prospect of conviction, and whether it is in the public interest to proceed with the prosecution. The Code for Crown Prosecutors, a freely available public document, explains the criteria that a prosecutor applies in making this decision.

Advance information

If the offence alleged is either way (see page 69), the prosecutor may at this stage prepare advance information, that is a summary of the evidence or copies of prosecution statements, which are served on the defendant, or his solicitor if he has one. Advance information provides some details of the prosecution case, although it is unlikely to consist of all the evidence and police records which would normally amount to the disclosure required before trial. Its purpose is to enable the defendant to decide (on advice if necessary) whether to have the charge heard at the magistrates' court or the Crown Court.

A well organised defendant will not be idle during this period. He or she may instruct a firm of solicitors or at least obtain legal advice as to the charge, and will probably apply for legal aid. If so forms will have to be signed and supporting information provided to enable the magistrates' court to consider the application in accordance with the legal aid regulations. This sometimes takes time, and although it should always be possible to make some progress at the first court hearing, in many cases no information has been served, legal aid has not been considered, or the defendant has done absolutely nothing and the case has to be put back in the court list, or even adjourned. There are those who would prefer to revert to the old system of bailing to the first available court date, in order — so it is argued — for the court to take control of the proceedings immediately. This would mean that persons such as drink/drivers who are unlikely to be granted legal aid can be dealt with much more quickly, and those found guilty can be disqualified much sooner, thereby offering the public the protection that is needed. It is arguable that the police could, when granting bail after charge, impose a condition that a defendant should not drive during the bail period, but that is a blanket approach which is not justified within the Bail Act provisions (see Chapter 8). The police cannot impose such a bail condition unless satisfied that without it there is a real risk that the defendant will offend whilst on bail. In practice it is unlikely that there is much to be gained by short bail periods, although from time to time a police force tries such a scheme, usually limited to persons charged with certain categories of offences.

Summonses

We have considered two ways in which a defendant may be brought before a court: the arrest with warrant and the arrest without warrant followed by charge. The third mechanism is the issue of a summons. This is by far the most common form of process. In theory it may be used in any sort of case, but in practice it is confined to the vast majority of road traffic cases, minor criminal matters, most prosecutions by local authorities for breaches of planning and other environmental matters — in fact the vast bulk of the work of magistrates' courts. The procedure is long-standing and arcane. The person seeking to bring the prosecution to court will 'lay an information' in person or by post at the court, and a justice of the peace or justices' clerk will consider it. An information should contain short particulars of what the defendant is said to have done, including the date and place, and identify the statute which it is alleged has been contravened. If the breach is of subordinate legislation, that authority should also be cited. Only one breach may be contained in an information; more than one allegation in a single information will render it 'bad for duplicity', a concept explained *in extenso* in a mass of case law. Charges as well as informations in summonses can be 'bad for duplicity'.

The general rule is that an information must be laid within six months of the alleged offence, although certain statutes may grant longer. Again, the law attaches importance to proceedings being taken with reasonable expedition, and summonses have been refused where the prosecutor leaves the laying of the information to the last permissible day without good reason. Issuing a summons is a judicial act, and the justice or justices' clerk is required to scrutinise the information to ensure that all the required information is given and that it is in time. If so, a summons will issue, addressed to the defendant, containing details of the allegation and naming a date, place, and time when the defendant is required to attend court. To be effective there must be proof that a summons has been properly served, i.e., that the defendant has received it. This is done by a certificate on the court's copy. Good service is effected by:

— delivering it to the person to whom it is directed ('personal service');

— leaving it for him with some person at his last known or usual place of abode;

— sending it by post in a letter addressed to him at his last known or usual place of abode.

Without proof of proper service, the court must assume the defendant does not know about the proceedings and is therefore unable to proceed in the absence of the defendant.

First appearance in court

If all has gone well, there is no reason why the case should not be concluded on the first appearance of the defendant in court. We have noted that the defendant will almost certainly have been told of the right to apply for legal aid, but even if the defendant has not done so there is almost always be a duty solicitor at court who is there for the express purpose of advising unrepresented defendants about their cases. Thus, for the sake of ten minutes' worth of advice, the defendant may have a clear indication as to whether (in an appropriate case) to elect trial by jury or consent to trial in the magistrates' court, and if summary trial is chosen, how to plead. Duty solicitors are practitioners who take their turn in assisting the courts in this way. They are paid at legal aid rates for their duty. Some busy courts will have more than one, and some will have a custody duty solicitor for those appearing unrepresented from custody, and a bail duty solicitor to represent those who have been granted bail by the police to appear at court. An experienced duty solicitor is invaluable to a busy court. More is said about duty solicitors in Chapter 11.

Asserting control

The most important thing a court can do is to assert control over the progress of the case from the very first moment the case appears in the list. It is the court which should control the proceedings, not the parties, and the importance of proper case management, consistent with the overriding need to do justice in each case, requires that at every appearance some progress towards the conclusion of the case should be made. This obliges courts to question — if necessary with vigour — every application for an adjournment and, if an adjournment is necessary, to adjourn for the minimum time necessary to enable the reason for the adjournment to be achieved. National pre-trial time limits for each stage of court proceedings have been agreed and the periods specified in them are to be regarded as maxima, but they do not have the force of law. Often it is possible for the purpose of the adjournment to be achieved in a significantly shorter timescale, with no detriment to any party. In many cases it can be achieved by setting the case back in the court list for, e.g., advice to be given or documents considered. The most important advice with regard to adjournments is that there is no such thing as an agreed adjournment between prosecution and defence. The court must always be convinced that it is in the interests of justice to delay cases. Deciding whether or not to grant a request for an adjournment is considered further in Chapter 10.

Mode of trial

Let us assume that the prosecution and defence are ready to make progress on the first appearance. What happens? When the defendant has been called and his or her name, address and age have been confirmed, the charges will be read by the legal advisor. In other words the advisor will take the court copy of the charge sheet or the informations and read them aloud to the defendant. If the matters are summary only, on each information being put, the defendant will be invited to plead guilty or not guilty. The plea will come from the defendant personally, although it is not uncommon for an advocate to prompt the defendant. If the defendant pleads not guilty, a date will be fixed for trial. The court will wish to know the number of witnesses likely to be called and any anticipated complexities so that an appropriate amount of precious court time can be allotted. Subject to the scheme of disclosure contained in the Criminal Procedure and Investigations Act 1996, the defendant is entitled not to give information which may disclose the defence, but is expected to assist the court on matters which may affect the length of the trial, such as whether it is likely that interview tapes will have to be played instead of a summary being read to the court, whether there is a substantial legal argument, or whether the court will be invited to visit the scene of the alleged incident. A date will be fixed by the court, and the defendant will be bailed to that date, or the case may simply be adjourned to that date for the defendant to attend again then. If the defendant pleads guilty, the facts are given, as described below.

In the case of an indictable only matter, a date will be fixed for committal, usually between four and eight weeks from the date of the first appearance, and the defendant will be remanded, either in custody or on bail, to that date. No plea is taken from the defendant. Assuming that there is enough evidence to put the defendant on trial, a plea will not be taken until the indictment is read at the Crown Court.

In the case of offences triable either way, the mode of trial decision is taken after the defendant has been identified. The prosecution will make representations as to whether the offence(s) should be tried at the Crown Court or by the magistrates. The defendant, through his or her advocate if represented, may then make representations in the matter, or may choose to make no representations. Until recently, how a defendant might plead was not relevant at the mode of trial stage. However, as a result of amendments made by the Criminal Procedure and Investigations Act 1996, a defendant may, before the magistrates determine mode of trial, give an indication that he will plead guilty. If so, the magistrates will proceed to deal with the matter, retaining their power to commit the defendant to the Crown Court for sentence in cases where their powers are considered insufficient. Where the defendant is unable or unwilling to give an indication of a guilty plea, the magistrates decide where the case should be tried. There are National Mode of Trial Guidelines which will assist them in their task. These are worth considering at some length, because they are a helpful means of assuring consistency of approach between benches in what may be a very important decision.

The law and the guidelines

In making the decision, the court must first apply *the law*. Section 19, Magistrates' Courts Act 1980 requires the court to have regard to:

— the nature of the case;
— whether the circumstances make the offence one of a serious character;
— whether the punishment which a magistrates' court would have power to inflict for it would be adequate;
— any other circumstances which appear to the court to make it more suitable for the offence to be tried in one way rather than the other;
— any representations made by the prosecution or the defence.

The guidelines include general observations, and guidance relating to specific offences. The general observations include advice such as:

— the court should never make its decision on the grounds of convenience or expedition;
— the court should assume for the purpose of deciding mode of trial that the prosecution version of the facts is correct;
— the fact that the offences are alleged to be specimens is a relevant consideration; the fact that the defendant will be asking for other offences to be taken into consideration, if convicted, is not.

A preamble to the guidance relating to specific offences is:

Cases should be tried summarily unless the court considers that one or more of the following features is present in the case and that its sentencing powers are insufficient. Magistrates should take account of their powers under s. 25, Criminal Justice Act 1991 to commit for sentence.

The specific features of relevance when dealing with allegations of theft or fraud are as follows:

— breach of trust by a person in a position of substantial authority, or in whom a high degree of trust is placed;

— theft or fraud which has been committed or disguised in a sophisticated manner;

— theft or fraud committed by an organised gang;

— the victim is particularly vulnerable to theft or fraud (e.g., the elderly or infirm);

— the unrecovered property is of a high value.

Appropriate guidelines are given for all the main categories of offences. The magistrates will consider the representations in the light of the guidance, make their decision and announce it. If they decide that the matter is too serious to be dealt with before them, they will adjourn for the preparation of committal papers (for an explanation of committal proceedings see page 78). If they consider the matter suitable for summary trial, that is not the end of the matter. The clerk will tell the defendant that he or she has the choice of where to be tried and that if the defendant consents to be tried by the magistrates, he or she retains the right to commit to the Crown Court for sentence if, in the course of hearing the case, the magistrates consider that the offence seems to be more serious than it at first appeared. This occurs most often when a defendant's criminal record, which is never disclosed when the mode of trial is being decided, aggravates the criminal conduct under consideration. The defendant thus has a free choice: to elect trial by jury, or to consent to summary trial. If trial at the Crown Court is elected, the case will be adjourned for the preparation of committal papers. If the defendant consents to summary trial, then pleas are taken, although, as has been explained, the defendant may already have chosen to give an intimation that he or she will plead guilty. If the defendant pleads not guilty, a hearing is fixed at which witnesses will be called; if the defendant pleads guilty the court will invite the defendant to sit down and the facts are then given.

Pleas of guilty

Outlining the facts

The prosecutor will give the facts of the case to the court. It is rare that this is more than a brief summary of what the defendant is alleged to have done, including the defendant's reaction when arrested and/or questioned about the offence. It may well go to the credit of the defendant when the defendant's sentence is decided if it can be shown that the defendant showed contrition at an early stage, and indicated readiness to admit responsibility for the crime. If the defendant wishes for other similar matters to be taken into consideration ('TICs'), those matters are then put before the court, and the clerk will ask whether the defendant accepts responsibility for each TIC, and wishes the court to have it taken into consideration on sentence. The convention allowing a defendant the opportunity to have similar matters taken into consideration saves the police the expense of preparing a full prosecution file on each offence, which would be required if each offence were separately charged. It thus saves time and money. There is no requirement for the defendant to accept the TICs, but the advantage of doing so is that it wipes the slate clean. If the defendant refuses to accept them, the police have a choice between bringing separate charges or taking no further action.

Compensation

Details will also be given of any financial loss arising from the crime, e.g., the cost of repairs to the window broken or the amount of money stolen from the employer's till. It is well established law that compensation is payable to cover loss up to a theoretical maximum of £5,000 but, as is seen in Chapter 9, the court must always have regard to the ability of the offender to pay, and if a compensation order is payable by instalments then it should normally be capable of payment within about 12 to 18 months. Compensation orders should be made only in respect of readily quantifiable amounts. If there is a real dispute between the offender and the victim either as to liability to pay compensation or the amount that should be ordered, and the dispute seems to be incapable of resolution after the hearing of brief evidence, it is preferable for the magistrates' court to make no order, and for separate proceedings to be brought by the victim in the county court to determine liability and amount.

Finally, the prosecutor will put the defendant's previous criminal record before the court. It is for the court to determine whether any entries on the list of previous convictions aggravate the latest offence. It is helpful to all parties if the court gives an indication as to whether or not they are considered to be aggravating. It will certainly help the defence advocate in his plea in mitigation.

Mitigation

When the prosecutor has finished and sits down, it is the opportunity for the defendant to mitigate the offence. But first, it is important that the court understands that the defence accepts broadly what the prosecution said in outlining its case. In many cases there are one or two minor facts which the defendant does not accept, but these are peripheral and they will have no effect on sentence. However, there are some cases where the defendant, although admitting responsibility for the crime, substantially disputes the facts. The defendant may accept that he or she assaulted the victim, but may say the assault consisted only of a punch or a slap with the flat of the hand. The victim may allege that the injuries were caused by a weapon. If there is a substantial discrepancy which is likely to have an effect on sentence, then the court will hold a special hearing after plea ('a *Newton* hearing') in which witnesses will be called on behalf of both prosecution and defence and the court will make findings of fact. The clerk will take a note of these findings of fact, and the bench will announce them. It is on the basis of facts which the prosecution has proved beyond reasonable doubt that the court will sentence the defendant. The *Newton* hearing is comparatively rare but of growing importance.

The first task that the defence will have is to try to gauge how the court will look at the prosecution facts, and whether to request the court to obtain a pre-sentence report. If the court is amenable to such a request, mitigation is usually left until the report is available. If it is not a case for reports the defence advocate will tackle the mitigation straightaway. This usually falls into two parts: mitigating the facts of the offence to try to show that it was less serious than might otherwise appear; and then mitigating the personal circumstances of the offender. This may take the form of drawing attention to the defendant's usual upstanding behaviour, good work record, and the wholesome interests that he or she follows for church or community, or it may dwell on the sad personal circumstances from which the defendant suffers, stress, illness, straitened circumstances etc. The magistrates will consider their sentence, often after deliberation in the retiring room, and will come back into court and pass sentence.

Summary trial

If the defendant has pleaded not guilty, then a trial must take place. Evidence will be given before the court, and after that, and speeches from the advocates, the magistrates will decide whether the defendant is guilty of the matter before the court. The speeches of the advocates are not evidence, but should be of assistance to the court in identifying the issues in the case and directing the court (and the legal advisor) to matters of law which are likely to arise. In the magistrates' court, it is usual for the prosecution to have the first word by opening the case to the court, and the defence to have the last word in its final address to the bench. Some variation is permitted to cater for different circumstances, but we shall stick to the general rule here.

The prosecution case

The prosecutor should tell the court simply and without repetition what the case is about and how it is said that the defendant is guilty of the offence charged, and may then outline what evidence it is intended to call (or read) to try to satisfy the burden on the prosecution to prove the defendant's guilt. Although there are occasions when the defendant has an evidential burden in a particular case, the 'golden thread' in the English criminal law is that the prosecution must prove the defendant's guilt, and to a standard that the court is *sure* of his guilt. The prosecution will then call its evidence. There are three ways of adducing evidence before the court:

— the calling of oral evidence;
— the service of written statements under s. 9, Criminal Justice Act 1967;
— formal admissions under s. 10, Criminal Justice Act 1967.

We shall consider each of these on pages 75–8.

Submission of no case

After the prosecution evidence is before the court, the defence will assess whether the defendant has a 'case to answer', and if not, may ask the court to dismiss the case at that point. The court of its own volition can assume that role, but must give the prosecutor the opportunity to explain the way in which the evidence before the court constitutes a case to answer. A hypothetical test is applied at that stage: could a reasonable bench, properly directing itself as to the law, and in the absence of any contrary evidence find the defendant guilty of the offence charged? If the answer is 'yes' the case will go on, if the answer is 'no', then the case will be dismissed then and there. There are a number of authorities to which a legal advisor might be expected to direct the bench in consideration of a submission of no case. Of course, the prosecutor may at any time up to that point offer no further evidence if the witnesses have not come up to proof.

The defence case

If there is a case to answer, the defence may elect to call no evidence, in which case the bench will have to decide whether *this bench* is sure of the defendant's guilt. In other words the theoretical test has now become specific to this bench's assessment of the evidence against this defendant in this case, and there may be the power to draw an adverse inference against the defendant because of his or her failure to testify. More often the defendant will give evidence, and as with the prosecution witnesses this evidence will be subject to examination in chief, cross examination and re-examination. Most witnesses are witnesses of fact, but there are exceptions, such as expert witnesses and character witnesses, who fulfil a different function from that of a witness of fact, but whose evidence will be scrutinised by the court in exactly the same way. At the end of the defence case, the defence advocate will address the court, drawing attention to the limitations of the prosecution case and inconsistencies between the witnesses. Just as it is valuable to have the first word at the beginning of a trial, it is undeniable that it is equally beneficial to have the final word before the bench goes out to consider whether or not the prosecution has proved the defendant's guilt.

Types of evidence

Oral evidence

The most common form of evidence in the magistrates' court is oral evidence given from the witness box. Generally, after an incident has taken place, the police or other investigating authority take a statement from each witness, and it is those statements, sometimes supplemented by additional statements, which form the basis of the 'proof' from which the prosecutor will examine the defendant. Evidence which is formal or uncontroversial will probably be served or admitted (see below) so that oral evidence normally deals with issues of fact which are in dispute between the prosecution and defence.

Witnesses in criminal trials wait outside the courtroom before giving evidence, and are called in at the request of the advocates at the appropriate time. They are present to give their accounts of the incident in question, and it is considered that those accounts are more likely to be accurate if untainted by what an earlier witness may have said. The defendant, of course, remains in court throughout the trial and hears everything that is said. The general rule is, however, that if the defendant chooses to give evidence he or she will do so before defence witnesses, who remain outside until called. Occasionally it happens that a witness has remained in court before giving evidence and has heard the testimony of earlier witnesses. The court should not refuse to hear that witness's evidence, but, when assessing the accuracy of what he or she has said, may take account of the fact that he or she has been in court and heard other witnesses.

Except in the case of a child witness, who will give unsworn evidence, all witnesses must give evidence either on oath or affirmation, and indeed the prospective witness has the right to take the oath on the holy book of his or her choice. If the witness has no religion, the taking of an oath is contrary to the witness's religion, or it is impracticable to administer the oath, for example because the appropriate holy book is not readily available, the witness will affirm. An affirmation carries exactly the same authority as an oath, and the days are gone when there was an enquiry as to why an individual wished to affirm. It is sometimes the case that through error a witness takes an oath on a book which may not be the holy book of the witness's religion, e.g., a Sikh may have taken the oath on the Bible, but that does not in any way invalidate or cast doubt on the evidence given, provided that the witness in fact regarded himself or herself as being bound by the oath that was taken. If a witness refuses to take either an oath or an affirmation, the witness is liable to be fined or imprisoned by the court. Such conduct is rare.

The witness will be examined, cross examined, and re-examined and then may be asked questions by the court, though the court should ask questions only to clarify matters which are unclear. The court should not rejoice in its own perspicacity by starting a line of questioning which the advocates have not pursued: there may be very good reasons why certain questions have been left unasked, and such an exercise may well tend to show partiality between the parties, which is to be avoided. The general rule is that the court should not 'enter into the arena' but should let the parties conduct the case. At the end of the evidence, it is a courtesy to thank the witness for giving evidence. The witness should then remain in the courtroom for the remainder of the case. However, it is becoming more common for the party calling the witness to ask the court's permission to 'release' the witness. If the court agrees, the witness may leave the building, perhaps with a word of reminder that the case should not be discussed with anyone who may be waiting to come into the witness box.

Evidence served under s. 9, Criminal Justice Act 1967

Written evidence in the magistrates' court is almost certainly governed by this section, and it is one regrettable feature of litigation in the summary courts that affidavit evidence (i.e. a sworn, written statement of fact) has never been introduced there. It would be a very inefficient use of court time if, in every case, no matter how trivial and whether the defendant attended or not, for a witness to have to attend to give oral evidence. It would be unsatisfactory both for members of the public who may lose time from work as a result of their civic-mindedness, and for police officers, ambulance personnel and others who could find themselves hanging round court buildings waiting to be called to give what might be uncontroversial evidence. This section allows a copy of a signed statement in the prescribed form to be served on the other parties to the proceedings, and to be read at the court hearing and thus be admissible in evidence in the same way as oral evidence would be, provided that none of the parties or their solicitors, within seven days from the service of the copy of the statement, serves a notice on the party proposing to adduce it, objecting to the statement being tendered in the evidence under the section. If there is an objection, the prosecution should call the witness or do without him or her. If there is no objection, then the evidence is read aloud by the party adducing it and the court considers that evidence along with all other evidence laid before it in the case. It follows that although it is more often the prosecution who make use of the s. 9 procedure, it is applicable to any party to the proceedings.

Admissions: s. 10, Criminal Justice Act 1967

It is the general rule that the prosecution is obliged to prove every element in its case against the defendant, and indeed in some cases strict proof of all parts of the allegation is required. But in most cases it is very plain where the dispute between the parties lies. For example in a case of careless driving, it may be that the defendant does not dispute that he was the driver, nor that he was driving on a road, but the issue in dispute is whether he drove without due care and attention. Or in a case of theft from a supermarket, it may not be in dispute that the defendant walked out of the store, nor that he failed to pay for the items the subject of the charge: the issue in dispute was whether he intended to steal.

This section allows for matters which are unlikely to be in dispute between the parties to be formally admitted. Certain conditions are laid down for the satisfactory operation of the section, but the gist is:

> ... any fact of which oral evidence may be given in any criminal proceedings may be admitted for the purpose of those proceedings by or on behalf of the prosecutor or defendant and the admission by any party of any such fact under this section shall as against that party be conclusive evidence in those proceedings of the fact admitted.

It is somewhat surprising that greater use is not made of this provision, but in reality a number of *informal* admissions are made in almost any trial. Without them the wheels of justice would certainly grind to a halt.

Committal proceedings

Committal proceedings take place in respect of indictable only offences which must be tried at the Crown Court and either way offences where the defendant has elected to be tried at the Crown Court (see page 69). They must be distinguished from a criminal trial. They do not determine an accused's guilt or innocence, but are an examination to decide whether or not there is a *prima facie* (sufficient) case against the defendant. In essence this means evidence on which, unless contradicted, a reasonable jury, directed as to the law, could properly convict. If there is a *prima facie* case, the court will commit the defendant to the Crown Court for trial. If not, the defendant will be discharged. Note that the charge is not dismissed and the distinction is not without importance. If further evidence comes to hand, a prosecution may be recommenced; if after a trial a charge is dismissed, the prosecution is precluded from proceeding a second time. So a committal hearing is an examination, and is conducted by an examining magistrate; one magistrate, lay or stipendiary will suffice, though most committals appear in a normal petty sessional court list, and take their turn with all the other work.

Committals without consideration of the evidence: s. 6(2), Magistrates'
Courts Act 1980

These are by far the most common form of committal proceedings and
require the defendant to be represented for them to take place. The
proceedings themselves are little more than a paper exercise, although
ancillary applications, such as whether or not the person committed
should be granted bail or committed in custody, require appropriate
consideration. The basis of committal without consideration of the
evidence is that the prosecution prepares a bundle of witness statements
in a prescribed form and a copy is sent to defence solicitors and the court.
The defence has the opportunity to read the evidence and consider
whether or not there appears to be a *prima facie* case against the client.
If there is, the defence will consent to a s. 6(2) committal and, when the
matter is listed in the magistrates' court, will indicate that fact and that it
does not wish to make submissions at that stage. The bundle of original
statements is handed into the magistrates' court and the legal advisor will
check the statements ready for their despatch to the Crown Court. The
defendant is then formally committed in custody or on bail to the Crown
Court to appear at a plea and directions hearing on a specified date,
usually in four to six weeks.

The plea and directions hearing is what it says. The defendant will be
expected to indicate a plea and in the event of a guilty plea will be dealt
with as soon as possible. If the defendant indicates that the plea will be
not guilty, the judge will give directions on a wide range of matters, and
these will be considered binding on prosecution and defence. It is outside
the scope of this work to go into further detail on this, but the laudable
purpose of such hearings is to enable the Crown Court to become
involved with the case at an early stage, and manage its progress, making
optimum use of court time and preventing unnecessary delay and
expense.

Committals after consideration of the evidence: s. 6(1), Magistrates'
Courts Act 1980

If the bundle served by the prosecution and considered by the defence is
thought not to contain a *prima facie* case against the defendant, the
defence will wish to make submissions on the inadequacy of the case.
Until the Criminal Procedure and Investigations Act 1996, it was possible
for witnesses to be called to give oral evidence at committal proceedings,

and the defence could call evidence if it wished to do so. Oral evidence at committal proceedings, whether from prosecution or defence, has now been abolished. Now there may be submissions that the evidence served, when taken together, does not amount to sufficient evidence to put the defendant on trial, or that in law sufficient evidence of the offence alleged is not provided. If the defence submission succeeds the defendant will be discharged, subject to the power of the court at committal proceedings to commit for any indictable offence disclosed on the face of the statement or depositions. If the submission is rejected, the defendant will be formally charged and committed in the same way as if it were a committal without consideration of the evidence.

In the mid 1990s, the Government legislated to replace committal proceedings with a streamlined system known as transfer for trial. This proved so problematical when the drafting of rules was considered that the measure was abandoned. The changes brought about by the 1996 Act are designed to make committal proceedings more effective, and look like achieving that end. There can be no doubt that, if used properly, they can prove a very effective filter for throwing out inherently weak cases at an early stage.

Notebooks and codes of practice

It is essential that the old (pre-1948) concept of police courts should have no relevance in the operation of contemporary magistrates' courts. Magistrates must be even-handed and be seen to be even-handed to all people coming before the courts. One issue on which members of the public have concerns is the use by police officers of notebooks from which they give their evidence with permission of the court. In fact, any witness is entitled to note what he or she saw of an incident and, provided the note is contemporaneous (which is given a wide interpretation), will be allowed to refresh his or her memory from it. What no witness should be allowed to do is to repeat verbatim what is written in the note or the notebook. It may sometimes stretch credulity, but the purpose of the note is to stimulate the memory, and not replace it. The average police officer will deal with a large number of matters between the incident leading to the appearance in court and the court hearing at which he or she is required to give evidence, often many months or sometimes even years later. It follows that the officer's memory of the incident concerned might be extremely sketchy without the ability to refer to a contemporaneous note.

It is important that there should not be an assumption by the court that the police officer will take out the book and start to refer to it. The prosecutor should ask some preliminary questions about the making of the note, and then seek the permission of the court to allow the officer to refer to it. A notebook containing particulars of an incident may be a potent weapon in the prosecution's armoury, but, as with many other aspects of the investigation process, detailed rules exist to protect the public. There was a danger, until the enactment of PACE, that a defendant might be 'verballed', i.e., untrue admissions put into his mouth by an unscrupulous police officer. There have no doubt been convictions secured in this way. Concerns about police powers led to PACE, which, as well as giving extra powers to the police, imposed codes of practice on them which they are obliged to follow. Under one of the codes, a police officer seeking to rely on evidence of admissions noted in his or her book would have to allow the suspect to read the notes (or, if unable to read, to have them read over) and then append a certificate at the end of the notes agreeing them to be a true record or not as the case may be. In addition, most police stations now have a special time clock which enables a printed and accurate record to be kept of precisely when notes were completed.

Codes of practice are not themselves law, but are made under the authority of PACE, and provide appropriate working standards for the police and other investigating agencies, which should ensure that the investigation is fairly conducted. There are five codes, made under s. 66, PACE:

— statutory powers of stop and search (code A);
— searching of premises and seizure of property (code B);
— detention, treatment and questioning of persons (code C);
— identification of persons (code D);
— tape recording of police interviews (code E).

Each of the codes is a public document and is freely available from HMSO, and reproduced in most of the reference books on criminal law. Many trials turn on whether the provisions of the relevant code have been followed or not. The status of the codes is that a breach of them by a police officer does not of itself render that officer liable to criminal or civil proceedings, though it may lead to disciplinary proceedings. Equally important is the power of the court in its discretion to exclude evidence which is shown to have been obtained as a result of a provision of one of the codes being breached. The court has considerable authority and discretion. In PACE itself there are sections dealing with the exclusion of confessions unfairly or oppressively obtained (s. 76), or unfair prosecution evidence (s. 78), and even after the enactment of PACE the court still retains common law powers to exclude evidence if it considers that it would be unfair to the accused to admit it.

The codes contain substantial written material and in some regards could be considered a counsel of perfection, so it may not be that every breach — however marginal — will lead to evidence being excluded. However, a breach or a number of breaches which are 'significant and substantial' will normally lead to a court taking the decision to exclude. The application of PACE and the Codes is universal throughout courts having criminal jurisdiction, and magistrates are obliged to consider and rule on these matters when raised in the course of a trial, but evidence cannot be excluded under ss. 76–78 of PACE in contested committal proceedings.

The prosecution or defence may, however, take the view that the matters discussed in this paragraph are often more felicitously dealt with in the Crown Court where there is a clear distinction between the roles of the judge and the jury. Issues of admissibility of evidence ('PACE points') are dealt with by the judge in the absence of the jury and evidence excluded is never put before the jury. In the magistrates' court justices both determine facts and rule on law, so that the 'offending' material is put before them as part of the legal argument to exclude. If the evidence is excluded they then have to perform mental gymnastics in putting it from their minds.

There are no doubt those who feel that the codes of practice err too much on one side or the other, but overall they may be thought to provide a fair balance between the need for thorough and vigorous investigation of what may be serious crimes and the need for suspects' rights to be safeguarded and for suspects to be dealt with fairly according to open and verifiable procedures.

The court and the legal advisor

It can be seen that the prosecution of offences and court hearings of criminal matters have a vast body of law attached to them, and no magistrate, however experienced, is able to obtain more than a working knowledge of the rules under which the criminal process operates. However, magistrates have the great benefit of being able to turn to a legal advisor (still sometimes called a 'court clerk') for advice on the law, and the practice and procedure of the court. Many are legally qualified as barristers or solicitors, and others have a Home Office diploma entitling them to be court clerks. The standards of all legal advisors have risen immeasurably during the last 20 years or so, and magistrates can generally have confidence that the advisor with them will know the answer to a point that crops up, or at any rate will know where to look, or failing that enlist the help of the justices' clerk who is ultimately responsible for the advice given.

It is most important to keep the functions of magistrates and legal advisor separate. Magistrates are there to decide the facts of the matter, and make decisions on points of law that may arise, and in an appropriate case, determine sentence. The legal advisor is just that — the court's professional advisor. There is no point in a bench asking the advisor whether he or she thinks the defendant drove carelessly because that is not the advisor's function, and a good advisor would politely decline to offer a view. Similarly, it would be wrong for an advisor to tell magistrates what sentence should be imposed. By doing so, he or she trespasses on the bench's function. What an advisor may do, and he or she may volunteer the information without waiting to be asked, is give the guidance of the Court of Appeal, or the local Crown Court liaison judge on sentencing offences of the same type, and remind the bench of whether there is any Magistrates' Association or bench guidance on the matter. This is not to put the court into a strait-jacket, but to enable the magistrates to have a general picture or 'ranging shot' as to where on the sentencing scale the offending conduct may come.

It can be seen that the functions of bench and advisor have a number of grey areas, even without considering the number of judicial functions which may be performed by the justices' clerk (see pages 54–5). There have been a number of Practice Directions to assist the smooth and fair running of the interaction between the two. The current one is the *Practice Direction (Justices: Clerk to Court)* [1981] 1 WLR 1163. This confirms the responsibility of the justices' clerk for the functions performed by any member of staff sitting in court as a legal advisor, and goes on to provide a framework for the responsibilities of the advisor in court.

The view is widely held that issues of law arising in the court during a trial and on which the bench requires advice should lead to the bench being given advice in open court. This enables the parties to hear the advice given, and in an appropriate case draw the court's attention to law or guidance that may have been omitted. When a court retires to consider its decision in a case, advice will be given by the legal advisor in the retiring room and thus will not be heard by the parties. However, if an issue of law or procedure arises during the court's deliberations which has not been canvassed during the hearing, it is submitted that the bench ought to return to court to hear argument on that point. This avoids the obvious peril of a bench deciding a case on law which has not been canvassed and which may be subject to argument.

Experienced magistrates and legal advisors are well aware of the parameters in which they are permitted to operate. In practice, there are few problems or concerns. The ideal arrangement marries the common sense and skills of the trained magistrate to the professional expertise of the advisor. A good test of how it works is to look at the relationship through the eyes of the impartial observer in the public gallery. If that individual perceives that the bench is making the decisions, assisted, where necessary, by the concise advice of its advisor, then the relationship is probably right. If, however, the legal advisor is running the proceedings, with a stance so proactive that the bench hardly gets a look in, then the perception will be that it is not a magistrates' court, but 'a magistrates' and advisor's court' or even 'an advisor's court' and the relationship is awry. Fortunately such a creation is rare indeed.

Magistrates and the criminal law

The subject of the criminal law is far too complex for a guide of this type, when extensive text and reference books are on the market. It is not advisable for justices to buy or read books on the criminal law. It is, no doubt, possible to acquire a passable knowledge of the law by reading books, but much foundation work needs to be done on issues such as fault requirements and general defences before individual offences can be properly understood. A little knowledge can be a dangerous thing in this field as in so many others.

It is very important that close attention is paid to the reading of the charge. What is universally known in convenient shorthand as 'threatening behaviour' contrary to s. 4, Public Order Act 1986 is, in fact, a most complicated offence capable of being committed in different ways and with different mental elements. Magistrates should not hesitate to have the charges read aloud in full at the beginning of a trial, or to ask advice from the legal advisor as to precisely what the prosecution has to prove. Shorthand descriptions of offences may be convenient, but it does not help in the court room context. The defendant pleading not guilty to 'shoplifting' cannot be found guilty unless the prosecution proves, so that the court is sure, that he or she 'dishonestly appropriated property belonging to another with the intention of permanently depriving the other of it'. Our convenient use of shorthand must not be allowed to obscure a precise, almost scientific, obligation. Magistrates should ask questions in court through their chairman, although as mentioned elsewhere in this chapter, it is important that no questions should be asked which demonstrate partiality or involve entering into the arena. But it is important that a bench knows what it is being asked to decide and it can discharge its duty only if it knows precisely. The role of the legal advisor is invaluable, but the advocates too, whether members of the Bar or solicitors, are under a duty to the court, and if an address or a submission obfuscates rather than simplifies, it is always permissible, through the chairman, for a magistrate to ask the advocate to clarify precisely what he or she is saying.

Six

Road Traffic Offences

Introduction

All magistrates deal with road traffic cases. Indeed more than 70 per cent of the workload in magistrates' courts is concerned with traffic, and this is despite legislation diverting many of the less serious traffic contraventions to the fixed penalty ticket procedure and away from the courtroom. There is a school of thought that finds traffic lists rather dull, and considers that it requires little more in sentencing terms than the application of the Magistrates' Association guidelines, suitably adjusted to cope with the merits of the case. A more informed view would point to the importance of the just enforcement of road traffic legislation, which exists to protect the road-using public from unsafe use of vehicles, whether through design, loading, maintenance, or the manner in which they are driven. Society is strangely complacent about the toll of road deaths and serious injuries. We are alarmed at the cost in human life when a plane crashes or a ship founders. These are big stories which command our attention and concern. We seem generally less concerned about those killed or badly hurt on the road, with the possible exception of the casualties in a mass pile-up in winter fog. The fact is that an average of ten people are killed on the roads every day in Great Britain, and many more are injured. We have far fewer road deaths than our neighbours in France and Germany, but an annual loss equivalent each year to the population of a large village or small town is unacceptable. We may refer to 'accidents', although in fact many road incidents are not accidents at all.

It is against that background that a magistrate should approach road traffic cases. The vast body of road traffic legislation and subordinate legislation (increasingly with its origins in Europe) has, as its principal aim, the protection of the road-using public from those who deliberately or through inadvertence would put it at risk. Fines, community sentences, imprisonment, endorsement and disqualification are some of the tools in the magistrates' armoury for dealing with traffic offenders. We shall consider these powers later.

Use/cause/permit

It is not always the driver or the owner of a vehicle who is responsible for it. Traffic law often penalises the 'user', or someone who has 'caused to be used' or 'permitted to be used' a vehicle on the road. It may not be necessary to look at those definitions in great detail, except to say that 'using a vehicle on a road' has a wide definition. In common parlance, if a person were referred to as 'using a car in the High Street', it would be assumed that he or she was driving it. But the technical way in which 'use' is interpreted in the legislation covers conduct which the man or woman in the street would not consider amounts to use. For example, a man buys a car and parks it on the road outside his house. He has decided not to drive it until he has bought insurance and had the vehicle tested. That person is guilty of the offences of using a vehicle without valid insurance, and using a vehicle without a current test certificate.

More than one person can be using a vehicle at the same time. For example, a driver of a company's lorry is travelling along a stretch of road when part of the load falls off. If proceedings are taken by the police for the use of a vehicle with an insecure load, the driver is regarded as a user, and so is the company provided that the vehicle is being used on company business, and the driver is not 'on a frolic of his own'.

'Causing' and 'permitting' have similar technical definitions: indeed ownership of a vehicle is seldom of any relevance. It will be recalled that a vehicle registration document deals with the 'keeper' of the vehicle, and it is the keeper who has various responsibilities when a vehicle is acquired or disposed of. As many private motor vehicles are owned by hire purchase companies or lease car fleet operators, it will be appreciated that ownership is usually unimportant.

For offences alleging bad driving, it is the driver, rather than the user or the owner, who will be prosecuted. It is possible to prosecute the owner where, for example, a lorry belonging to a company has been driven dangerously because of the state of the vehicle and its unlawful condition. In many instances, the police will see the driver at the scene of the incident complained of, but there are occasions where either the police are not called, or where the driver has failed to stop at the scene and the only details taken have been the registration number of the offending vehicle. In those circumstances, the police will carry out a check on the Police National Computer (PNC), where details of the registered keeper are held. A form is sent to the registered keeper, who is required to give particulars of the driver of the vehicle on the relevant occasion. If the information is not given, the keeper is liable to substantial penalties, including a fine, a mandatory endorsement of three penalty points, and a discretionary disqualification. It will be seen that this sort of methodical approach works adequately in the case of comparatively trivial offences, but is not fast enough to deal with an instance of failing to stop after an accident where it is suspected that the driver was also driving with excess alcohol. By the time the identity of the driver has been discovered, evidence of drink/driving has long since disappeared. It is one of the reasons why both Parliament and the courts have taken an increasingly serious view of motorists who fail to stop and/or fail to report an accident. A few years ago, the law was changed to provide the penalty of imprisonment for this category of case. It is hoped that the deterrent effect of this will persuade potentially errant motorists to face up to their responsibilities.

Tickets or court hearings?

Not all traffic contraventions come to court. It would be a ridiculous use of time and resources if the most trivial parking infringement saw the defendant required to attend and be dealt with by a bench of magistrates, but we have not reached a stage where the right — as opposed to the obligation — to attend court has been abolished altogether. We are not at the stage where, in the event of a contravention leading to a ticket being issued, one merely 'pays the traffic cop'. This is probably less to do with the thought that some policemen would be corrupt in their dealings with money obtained from motorists, than the traditional view that the enforcement arm of the law should remain separate from the judicial. Motorists issued with tickets (or 'fixed penalty notices' as they are properly called) can reflect for a few days on whether they consider themselves guilty or not. If guilty, the motorist can pay the ticket in person or by post to the office of the appropriate justices' clerk. If the motorist wishes to contest the matter, he or she can request a court hearing. At such a hearing evidence will be called and the bench will decide in the usual way whether the defendant is guilty or not. Just occasionally a motorist will wish to have a hearing to bring out particular items of mitigation which in his or her view might lead to the bench ordering some lesser penalty than a fine, such as an absolute or a conditional discharge.

Until the implementation of the Transport Act 1982, 'tickets' meant 'parking tickets' but the Act increased greatly the number of offences that could be dealt with in this way. The relevant law is now contained in Part III of the Road Traffic Offenders Act 1988. Speeding is a classic example. Provided that the motorist stopped after a speed check has his or her driving licence to hand and gives it to the police (speeding is, of course, an endorseable offence), the officer might be prepared to issue a fixed penalty ticket. The police have a discretion in this situation: they are not obliged to issue a ticket. The speed alleged may be substantially over the speed limit and therefore too serious to be dealt with by ticket; or an examination of the motorist's licence may reveal that he or she has previous endorsements and is therefore likely to receive a mandatory or discretionary endorsement at court. All tickets issued for endorseable offences carry three penalty points, but a case of speeding dealt with by the court carries a range of points between three and six depending on the court's view of the seriousness of the circumstances of the offence.

The fixed penalty system would be efficient and successful if those issued with a ticket either paid promptly or requested a court hearing so that the case could be determined in court. Unfortunately a great many people simply do nothing. The Transport Act 1982 brought in, for the first time, a system of what has been called 'guilty by inertia'. This gives power to the police, where the ticket remains unpaid and no hearing has been requested, to register the unpaid ticket as a fine at the offender's local court, or, where the offender was not seen at the time of the offence, at the registered keeper's local court. The unpaid ticket is enhanced in value by 50 per cent, so that a £40 ticket becomes a £60 fine, and a £20 ticket becomes a £30 fine. Such fines can be enforced in exactly the same way as any other fines. This is a system which, by and large, works satisfactorily although it depends — as in so much else concerned with the enforcement of traffic laws — on people who acquire or dispose of vehicles remembering to notify the DVLA of those changes.

If a motorist who is alleged to have committed offences is not proceeded against by ticket, for example where several traffic offences are alleged from the same incident, the police have two options. If there is a power of arrest, the suspect will be taken to the police station and, assuming it is felt that there is enough evidence to charge, he or she will be charged, and either bailed or not bailed but brought before a magistrates' court. This will be as soon as reasonably practicable, and in any event within 24 hours, not counting Sundays and certain bank holidays.

Much more common in traffic cases is that the suspect will be 'reported for consideration of prosecution'. This means that a report will be prepared by the investigating police officer, and this will be considered by a senior police officer, who will decide whether or not to prosecute. Prosecution is not automatic. Leaving aside the informal warning or advice given by the police officer at the roadside, the police may write to the suspect saying that no further action will be taken, or warning the person about his or her driving conduct. If the suspect is to be prosecuted, a rather old-fashioned procedure is followed. Instead of giving the motorist a notice of hearing with details of the allegation sufficient for the motorist to know what he or she faces, the police will *lay an information* with the magistrates' court for the petty sessional division where the offence is said to have taken place. Informations may be laid before a justice of the peace or a justices' clerk, and they are scrutinised to see whether the allegation is clearly stated and discloses an offence known to law. Judicial consideration has to be given, and although informations are for the most part considered in the absence of the prosecutor, the prosecutor may be asked to attend to clarify or justify the proposed prosecution.

If the statutory requirements have been complied with, the justice or justices' clerk will issue a summons, a document containing the allegations which the motorist will have to face, and giving the time, date and place at which he or she must appear.

The laying of an information sounds a ponderous procedure, and it is. It is not a formality, and the High Court has drawn attention on a number of occasions to the importance of the procedure being properly observed. But much of the work is now produced in computerised form, in other words the police prosecution department may lay hundreds or even thousands of informations in one computer print-out by direct link to the justices' clerk's office. The clerk will carefully cast an eye over the print-out and, if all appears in order, will issue the summonses.

The summonses then have to be served. There has been a wealth of law surrounding the service of summonses, but perhaps it will suffice to say here that the vast majority of summonses will be 'served', i.e., 'sent', by ordinary first class post. An alternative method is for summons to be 'personally served', i.e., hand delivered by a police officer or process server to the individual concerned. Another option is to leave it with an adult person at the individual's last known address.

Although the summons requires the attendance of the defendant, it is ironical that with the summons there will almost certainly be a wad of other papers telling the defendant that he or she need not, in fact, appear. This is the documentation relating to the 'guilty plea in absence' procedure, first introduced 40 years ago, and now very well accepted. There will be a 'statement of facts', which will give an outline account of what is alleged, for example:

> That at 09.30 on December 4th 1996, you were seen driving a motor vehicle in Whiteacre Road, Anytown. The speed of your vehicle was checked by police radar equipment and was found to be 65 mph. The speed limit for the relevant part of Whiteacre Road is 30 mph.

A recipient who intends to plead guilty will sign a form to the effect, and has the opportunity to write down any mitigating features, and give details of his or her financial circumstances. Although there is nothing to stop the defendant attending court and speaking in person, the purpose of the procedure is to excuse him or her from doing so. Some defendants still appear at the hearing, even though they have completed and sent back the relevant forms. If they do so they can take a normal part in the proceedings, and if they plead guilty, mitigate, either by asking the legal advisor to read out what was written earlier or by substituting or supplementing the written plea by oral comments.

The prosecutor, in this instance normally a police officer, may read aloud only the statement of facts and no elaboration is permitted. The legal advisor must then read to the court the defendant's mitigation and financial details, so that the bench has adequate information on which to base its decision. The defendant will also have been asked to produce his or her driving licence where the offence is endorseable, and the legal advisor will give details of the licence — and any endorsements and disqualifications recorded on it — when the prosecutor has read the statement of facts. If the bench proposes to disqualify the defendant either for the offence or because he or she is due for a 'totting up' disqualification, the defendant must be given notice of the fact. Most courts require the defendant to be physically present when a disqualification is imposed. Others do not, but in all cases the defendant must have received notice of the court's intention giving the defendant the option to attend to 'show cause' why disqualification should not ensue. The court can enforce the requirement to attend by the issue of a warrant, either with or without bail.

In all cases, the defendant will be notified of the outcome of a case dealt with under this procedure. Usually that will mean a fine notice, giving details of the fine and any costs imposed, and the rate of payment or the date by which it is ordered that the fine is to be paid. Where a licence endorsement has been ordered, details are sent to the Driver and Vehicle Licensing Authority (DVLA), which will later return the licence to the defendant at the address shown on the licence.

There are also cases in which the ticket procedure or the plea of guilty in absence procedure has not been thought appropriate. Then the summons will mean what it says, that the defendant must attend at the time, date, and place specified to answer the allegation. At one time the case would actually be heard on the date in the summons, and perhaps scores of witnesses would be waiting around on the off-chance that they might have to give evidence. If a defendant pleaded guilty their time was totally wasted. The treatment of witnesses and efficient use of expensive court time has now been improved, and in consequence the defendant will be dealt with on the return date only if he or she pleads guilty and, in the case of endorseable offences, has remembered to bring his or her driving licence. If the defendant pleads not guilty, a date will be fixed for trial. An estimate will be given of the likely length of hearing, non-availability dates for prosecution and defence witnesses are considered, and a date fixed. On that date, evidence will be heard and a decision made.

Bad driving offences triable by magistrates

As with other offences, traffic offences are divided between those which may be dealt with on indictment only; those which are triable 'either way'; and the vast majority which are summary only, that is, they can be tried only in the magistrates' court. Examples of the first category are causing death by dangerous driving and causing death by careless/ inconsiderate driving whilst over the limit etc. Dangerous driving can be tried either at the Crown Court or in the magistrates' court, i.e., it is an 'either way' offence. Speeding, careless driving, and construction and use offences may be tried summarily only.

As to bad driving offences, generally, the law has been made simpler and more effective as a result of the review of the relevant legislation which led to the implementation of the Road Traffic Act 1991. That Act touched many aspects of traffic work, but most importantly revised the law relating to bad driving offences.

Dangerous driving

If tried by the magistrates' court this offence carries a maximum of six months' imprisonment and/or a fine on Scale 5 (currently £5,000). It also carries an obligatory disqualification of a minimum of 12 months, and a disqualification until an extended driving test is passed. It follows that dangerous driving is intended to deal with really bad driving behaviour:

A person is guilty of dangerous driving if he drives a mechanically propelled vehicle dangerously on a road or other public place (s. 2, Road Traffic Act 1988).

The test of dangerous driving consists of an objective assessment of the defendant's driving. It is to be regarded as dangerous, if
[a] the way he drives falls far below what would be expected of a competent and careful driver, and [b] it would be obvious to a competent and careful driver that driving in that way would be dangerous (s. 2A(1), Road Traffic Act 1988).

'Dangerous' refers to danger either of injury to any person or of serious damage to property:

... regard shall be had not only to the circumstances of which the driver could be expected to be aware, but also to any circumstances shown to have been within the knowledge of the defendant. Further, a person is to be regarded as driving dangerously if it would be obvious to a competent and careful driver that driving a vehicle in its current state would be dangerous (s. 2A, Road Traffic Act 1988).

Careless driving

This offence is, as we have seen, triable only before magistrates. The relevant section of the Road Traffic Act 1988 creates offences of both careless and inconsiderate driving. There is considerable overlap between the two, and the penalties on conviction are identical. For inconsiderate driving (technically driving without reasonable consideration for other road users), there must be proof of a 'victim', i.e., someone actually inconvenienced by the driving:

> If a person drives a mechanically propelled vehicle on a road or other public place without due care and attention or without reasonable consideration for other persons using the road or place, he is guilty of an offence.

This is an offence which carries a maximum penalty of a fine on Scale 4 (currently £2,500), with a mandatory endorsement of between three and nine penalty points, and discretionary disqualification. Careless driving again requires an objective test, which might be defined as a departure from the standards of the reasonable, prudent, and competent driver in all the circumstances of the case. That paragon of driving virtue always drives with an appropriate level of competence whether there is a blanket of freezing fog, or it is a bright sunny day, and whether he or she be on city streets or in the depths of the country. There is no requirement that the defendant *fall far below* as in the case of dangerous driving, and, again unlike dangerous driving, the consequences of the driving are normally irrelevant. In assessing dangerous driving, a court may legitimately look at the consequences of what happened, for example that the offending vehicle struck a stationary vehicle, causing damage. With careless driving the focus is on the act of carelessness rather than on the consequences. Thus even if as a result of an act of carelessness a child was knocked from a cycle causing severe injuries, it is the carelessness rather than the injuries that are considered. This is one of the reasons that relatives of a person killed in an accident arising from an act of careless driving often feel aggrieved that 'her life was only worth £300' or whatever. Their sense of injustice is understandable, but is properly directed at Parliament rather than the courts. If consequences are to be taken into account in cases of careless/inconsiderate driving, it requires a change in the law to say so.

Drivers, drink and drugs

If the traffic legislation is there to protect and promote safety on the roads, then the physical condition of the driver must be an important focus. There are measures to guard against the old and infirm holding a licence when, owing to their medical state, or their diminished eyesight, they are unsafe to drive. The DVLA requires information about fitness on driving licence application forms, which have to be submitted annually by those who have attained the age of 70. Non-disclosure of relevant information about an individual's state of health is a serious offence. The courts too have power to disqualify a defendant until he or she has taken and passed a driving test if it is deemed necessary on the grounds of safety. The law in this respect is not directed exclusively at the elderly, but it is the elderly who are more often disqualified under this provision.

Over the last 30 years, much more stringent action has been taken against those who drive, or are in charge of, a vehicle, with excess alcohol, or whilst unfit to do so through drink or drugs. As conviction for an offence of driving with excess alcohol or whilst unfit leads to a mandatory minimum 12 months' disqualification, it is hardly surprising that much of the litigation in road traffic law in this period has surrounded the procedures used for ascertaining guilt.

When Barbara Castle piloted the Road Safety Bill through the Commons in 1967, there was concern in Parliament and in the country about the interference with personal liberty that the drink/driving procedure implied. That fear has diminished, particularly in the light of some very well publicised examples of deaths arising from accidents where one or more of those involved was 'over the limit'. Despite the huge publicity campaigns which are still promoted about the effects of drink and driving, it has been estimated that drink is a contributory factor in one third of all accidents.

It is important to realise that in the offence of driving whilst unfit the test is whether the suspect's ability to drive properly was impaired through either drink or drugs. Sometimes that is proved by direct evidence of the driver's condition: that the driver was unable to stand unaided, or slumped to the ground on getting out of the car, that a doctor at the police station certified the person unfit etc. The offence of driving with excess alcohol has nothing to do with 'being drunk'. It means that when tested, the proportion of alcohol in breath/blood/urine exceeded the prescribed level (35 microgrammes/80 milligrammes/107 milligrammes). Before a motorist can be requested to provide a specimen of breath for a test at the roadside, the police must have grounds for making the request, for example that the motorist is alleged to have committed a moving traffic offence, that he or she has been involved in an accident, or that there is reasonable cause to suspect that he or she has consumed alcohol. If the roadside test is positive, or if the suspect fails or refuses to provide a specimen and the police remain suspicious, then the suspect may be arrested and taken to the police station. It is there that the evidential procedure is carried out, usually by the requirement for the provision of breath tests (two in number), or if there is good reason for not asking for breath, then blood (taken by a doctor), or urine as the case may be. The suspect cannot choose what form of test to have, but can put forward medical reasons, such as the fact that he or she is suffering from asthma, which may make the provision of breath specimens impossible or dangerous. The police are obliged to take note of what the suspect says as to this, and if breath cannot be given, then the officer may request blood or urine.

The breath test equipment at the police station gives an instant result. If the suspect has given the two tests and the lower indicates that he or she has 35 microgrammes of alcohol or more, then he or she will almost certainly be charged with the offence there and then, and usually bailed to court. If however, the lower reading is in the range 35–50, the suspect can choose to have the breath tests replaced by a specimen of blood or urine. If blood, a doctor will be sent for and a sample of blood will be taken. It is divided into three, and the suspect will be given the choice of one of the three sealed containers. The suspect can then have the sample separately analysed if he or she so wishes. A second portion is retained by the police, and the third sent for forensic analysis. The suspect will normally be bailed to come back to the police station on a date when the results of the test are known. In the case of urine, a doctor is not involved. The suspect is required to provide two specimens within one hour. The first is discarded, the second — after being duly divided — is sent off for analysis.

Failure without reasonable excuse to provide specimens at the roadside (the screening test) is an offence carrying a fine on level 3 (currently £1,000), a mandatory endorsement with four points, and a discretionary disqualification.

Failure to provide evidential specimens without reasonable excuse is punishable in the same way as driving with excess alcohol/unfit through drink or drugs, with a maximum term of six months' imprisonment and/or a fine on level 5 (£5,000). This means that there is absolutely no advantage to a suspect who refuses to provide specimens. There is also a mandatory endorsement and a mandatory disqualification of a minimum of 12 months. If the offender is convicted of driving with excess alcohol, driving whilst unfit through drink or drugs, or failure to give evidential specimens, and has a previous offence in this category within the previous ten years, the minimum period of disqualification is three years.

There can be no doubt that the existence of these laws has made a substantial contribution to the safety of the road-using public, if not because of the fine that is the normal sentence passed by the court, but because of the disqualification that is the usual consequence of conviction. It is only in a very narrow range of cases, where the court finds that there are special reasons relating to the offence (not the offender), that it may exercise its discretion and not disqualify. As a large number of motorists need their licences for work, and without a licence it is impossible for them to do their jobs, the risk of being caught and then disqualified provides some deterrent. There is also a growing stigma attaching to the offence for reasons given previously. In the case of high readings of twice or three times the legal limit, courts will consider a community sentence, or even imprisonment. If there are aggravating features such as a high reading and an accident with damage and/or personal injury, a term of custody — though short — is often called for. In some parts of the country, the probation service has developed courses which may be 'bolted on' to probation orders. Typically, the course will require attendance once a week over ten weeks when the use and effect of alcohol, and the responsibilities towards others when alcohol is used, are explained. These are not just lectures, where the offender can sit in the corner and say nothing. Each individual is expected to confront his or her own behaviour and participate in the discussions which are a feature of such courses. Certain of these programmes have Home Office approval, and successful qualification on these will enable the offender to have a proportion of his or her disqualification remitted.

Construction and use offences

This rather daunting title covers a great many offences which again have the protection of the road-using public as the *raison d'être*. Increasingly, subordinate legislation in this branch of traffic law has its genesis in Europe where there is now considerable standardisation in the minimum specifications for many motor vehicle components. Several times each year, measures are passed importing into English law the latest weight restrictions on vehicles, technical specifications on brakes, or the approved dimensions of brake light clusters. Much of it is highly technical and is not of the greatest day-to-day importance to magistrates' courts.

More important than the construction of vehicles is the manner in which they are used, and, in particular, the law requires components of vehicles to be properly maintained in good and efficient working order: brakes, lights, tyres, steering etc. It also requires loads and fittings to be safely secured to the vehicle. The law is flexible enough to cater for matters of growing environmental concern: for example, prosecution for exceeding prescribed exhaust emissions may be brought.

Offences under the Road Vehicles (Construction and Use) Regulations 1986 are all triable summarily only, and can be divided into four separate categories.

Danger

If a person uses causes or permits a motor vehicle to be on a road, when (a) the condition of the vehicle etc. (b) the purpose for which it is used (c) the number of passengers carried or the manner in which they are carried (d) the weight, position, or distribution of its load or the manner in which it is secured ... is such that the use of the vehicle etc. involves a danger of injury to any person, he [or she] commits an offence.

The offence is endorseable with three points, or a discretionary disqualification. The maximum fine is on Scale 5 (if committed with a goods vehicle or a vehicle adapted to carry more than eight passengers); otherwise Scale 4 (s. 40, Road Traffic Act 1988).

Brakes, steering, tyres

Failing to comply with a construction and use requirement relating to brakes, steering and tyres is an offence endorseable with three points, or a discretionary disqualification. The maximum fine is as under 'danger' above.

Weight

Failing to comply with a construction and use requirement as to any description of weight applicable to a goods vehicle etc. is an offence, which is not endorseable or disqualifiable. The maximum fine is on Scale 5.

The remainder

This covers matters such as defective warning instruments (horns). The offence does not attract endorsement and/or disqualification. The maximum fine is on Scale 4, if committed in respect of a goods vehicle etc., and Scale 3 in any other case.

Driving whilst disqualified

One of the great problems facing courts dealing with the road traffic legislation is to ensure that their orders are followed. Non-payment of fines can be dealt with by enforcement procedures (see Chapter 9), but a substantial problem exists where motorists fail to respect an order of disqualification. Any flouting of the order of a court is to be deprecated, but the more so with driving whilst disqualified, because it is automatically the case that any policy of third party insurance held by the offender will be of no effect during the period of disqualification, putting the public at still greater risk. The offence of driving whilst disqualified is prevalent. At one time the offence was triable at the Crown Court, but for many years now it has been triable summarily only. At one time custody was almost inevitable, nowadays it is common, but often a community sentence is imposed. The offence requires proof of the disqualification (and there can be difficulties in proving that this defendant is the same individual who was disqualified at X court) and proof of driving. The offence carries a maximum sentence of six months and/or a fine on Scale 5. It is endorseable with six points, and carries a discretionary disqualification.

Endorsement and disqualification

Some offences, like highway obstruction, and using a vehicle in contravention of the lighting regulations, do not carry endorsement or disqualification, but for very many offences the court must endorse an offender's licence and has the discretion to disqualify. Other offences still require the court both to endorse and to disqualify. It is important to remember that the principal purpose of road traffic legislation is to promote road safety, and the power of courts to endorse licences and impose disqualifications gives effect to the requirement that persons convicted of serious offences, or those convicted of several less serious offences over a period of time, should forfeit their right to drive for a fixed period.

Assuming that the court has convicted an offender of an offence of exceeding the speed limit, the next task will be to order the production of the driving licence. The justices will decide whether the circumstances of the case require that the offender be disqualified for the offence. The offender may have driven at a very high speed in a built-up area, at a time of day when the roads and pavements are busy, and the court may decide, in addition to imposing an endorsement on the licence, to disqualify the offender on a discretionary basis. This power is available whether or not the offender has previous endorsements, and the period of the disqualification is wholly within the discretion of the court. Often for a first offence of this type, a disqualification of one month or less might suffice. The road-using public is protected from the offender's driving for that period of time. However, it may be that the speeding offence does not raise any particular concern, and a disqualification is not called for. In this situation, the court is obliged to endorse points on the licence. It will have a discretion for the offence of speeding to endorse a number of points in a range of between three and six.

Let us suppose that the court determines that four is the appropriate number. Those points are endorsed on the licence, and the DVLA is notified of that fact. The points will stay on the licence for four years, but will be effective for three. If the offender receives 12 or more points within a three year period, he or she must be disqualified from driving for a minimum of six months. The four points act as a warning to the offender to maintain good driving conduct or face the consequences of a ban. If, on requiring production of the licence, the court sees that in the three years prior to the date of the commission of the offence before it, the defendant already has, say, nine points the addition of the four that the court has determined should be imposed for the instant offence will mean that it must impose a minimum six months' disqualification. That period is, however, increased to one year if the defendant has had a previous disqualification for a fixed term of 56 days or more within the last three years, and to two years if there has been more than one such disqualification during that period. The purpose of this is to increase the penalties for 'cumulatively bad' driving.

If the offender is convicted of an offence which carries obligatory endorsement and obligatory disqualification, the court will not impose points, but will endorse the licence and then go on to disqualify the offender for a minimum of 12 months. If the offender has a previous similar conviction within a ten year period, an enhanced period of disqualification will apply.

Special reasons and mitigating circumstances

If the court is obliged to order the endorsement of a driving licence, it may in certain rare circumstances decide not to endorse where it finds there are special reasons for not doing so. In general terms, these must be clear mitigating features which do not amount to a defence to the charge, but which a court ought properly to take into account when arriving at a sentence. An example may be where a father broke a speed limit in rushing a sick child to the casualty department of the local hospital. There is no defence to the charge, but there is a genuine reason which a court ought properly to reflect in sentencing. If such a reason is accepted the court will not endorse, and that means the offender will receive no penalty points for that offence. If the offender would otherwise be liable to totting up, there will be no disqualification.

However, where an offender is liable to be totted up, there is a potential escape from totting up disqualification if he or she is able to convince the court that there are mitigating circumstances to justify either not disqualifying, or disqualifying for less than the appropriate period.

The law requires that before a court finds such mitigating circumstances, it must be shown that the offender would be caused *exceptional hardship* by the disqualification. The phrase is important. All disqualifications will result in some hardship to the defendant, but the hardship to be considered as mitigating circumstances here must be 'exceptional'. Unlike the plea of special reasons, which relates to the offence, exceptional hardship can relate to the defendant's personal circumstances: more often than not that the defendant would lose his or her job if the disqualification takes effect. It is important that the court scrutinises the evidence carefully. Does the plea depend on the defendant's own evidence? Has the employer come to court to give evidence about the potential loss of employment? If exceptional hardship is found, the court will have to determine whether there should be no disqualification or whether the term will be abbreviated. The legal advisor will note in the court register the precise findings of the court, because the offender will not be able to urge the same mitigating circumstances, should he or she be liable for totting up again within the three year period.

Special reasons for not endorsing/disqualifying may be pleaded in offences carrying obligatory disqualification, and these also are very tightly construed. Almost inevitably they arise in cases of excess alcohol and the defendant often says that his or her drink was laced, so that the defendant did not realise how much alcohol he or she was consuming.

Medical evidence to support the plea is almost certainly needed, and the law is not uncomplicated. In such a case the bench will need careful advice from their legal advisor, and it is outside the scope of this work to consider it here in greater detail.

Conclusion

It can be seen that, far from being dull and routine, road traffic work can be important and stimulating. The least satisfactory aspect concerns the small number of motorists who 'play the system', ignoring summonses, adjournment notices, and often warrants with bail. It can be months or even years before the court catches up with them, and thus in serious cases, persons who may represent a danger to the public and who should be disqualified are still driving.

The fault does not lie with the substantive law, which has developed with commendable logic and certainty, but rather with anachronistic procedural methods of securing attendance. Although opposed by the civil liberties lobby, the legal requirement for drivers to carry their driving licences would also be a considerable assistance in tightening up the enforcement of traffic laws, with consequent benefits to road safety.

Seven

Special Jurisdictions

Special jurisdictions in the magistrates' courts

Before we look at the special jurisdictions that magistrates have, we need to consider the meaning of 'special' jurisdiction in the petty sessions court. In a strict sense what we are about to examine is not 'special' at all but an integral part of petty sessional jurisdiction, not involving the police or the Crown Prosecution Service.

The man or woman in the street almost certainly still perceives the magistrates as dealing with police court work, although it is 50 years since the name of these courts changed from 'Police Court' to 'Magistrates' Courts', and it is as well to remind ourselves that although the police may be the best 'customers' of the magistrates' courts, their status within them is no different from, and no more important than, that of any other party. All magistrates must make sure that at each stage of their magisterial careers they keep the police (and other parties) at arm's length. It is easier to do justice, and to be seen to do justice, if this simple requirement is always observed.

Petty sessions work is not just about prosecutions brought by the police and taken over by the CPS; other governmental and non-governmental agencies may be regular prosecutors in court, and there remains the power of the ordinary citizens to institute and prosecute cases as 'private prosecutors'. As an example of non-police, non-CPS prosecutions, the Department of Social Security prosecutes a wide range of benefit frauds, ranging from comparatively small false claims where a defendant has claimed unlawfully when earning money, through to major frauds involving many defendants, considerable sophistication, and often an international element. The more serious prosecutions will certainly be committed to the Crown Court by the magistrates in exactly the same way as other serious crime.

HM Customs & Excise appear regularly, particularly if the magistrates' court is near a major airport or seaport. That department is also responsible for the administration and collection of VAT, and therefore VAT frauds may be prosecuted in any magistrates' court. More traditional customs work might consist of prosecution for evasion of excise duty on large amounts of liquor imported into the UK, or for illegal importation of drugs. In the latter cases, perhaps, couriers are intercepted on entering the country or parcels containing drugs are intercepted. All prosecutions will start in the magistrates' courts, and most of the importation cases will proceed through the usual committal procedure to the Crown Court.

Local authorities frequently bring cases before the courts. In the discussion of the family proceedings court (below) the role of local authorities in public law cases is considered, but in petty sessions courts they have a wide jurisdiction. This may range from prosecutions for unlawful harassment of a tenant or for the burgeoning problems of noise nuisance, through to enforcement of community charge arrears (now mercifully a diminishing problem) and for council tax non-payments. Breaches of planning regulations are often prosecuted by local authorities. The Inland Revenue, perhaps surprisingly, is entitled to come before the magistrates' court (rather than the county court) to recover as a civil debt amounts of income tax, due and payable, provided these amount to less than £1,000. Other regular prosecutors may be bus and railway companies, bringing cases for non-payment of fares or breach of by-laws.

It is also worth mentioning the right of gas and electricity suppliers to apply for warrants of entry. These are usually for the purpose of reading meters where access has not been possible in the usual ways, but also for disconnection of supply where there has been a history of non-payment. It can be seen that these are powers which need to be exercised with the greatest care, and although there may be applications for perhaps 40 or more similar warrants, it is important that individual attention is given to each. Both gas and electricity suppliers operate according to codes of practice, and when magistrates are hearing an application it is important to confirm that the relevant code of practice has been followed. If not, or if there is doubt whether it has, then the application should be refused.

Although there is an obvious desire to move through a list of applications in a businesslike way, it is important that time is taken to consider each application with appropriate care. The need to do justice is always more important than the battle against the clock.

This note of non-police prosecutors is not in any way exhaustive. A magistrate might turn up to a sitting to find that he or she is hearing a prosecution brought by the data protection registrar or by the RSPCA. All this work adds to the scope and interest of the jurisdiction of these courts of summary jurisdiction. It also confirms the need for magistrates to prepare properly for their work. This does not usually mean advance reading — although in the family proceedings court it frequently does — but it does mean arriving at the court in good time to be briefed by the legal advisor as to what unusual features the list might contain. Magistrates are almost all busy people with a range of commitments of which sitting in court is just one, but to be at court at least 15 minutes before the sitting of the court is always time well used.

We have spent most of our tour through the work of magistrates and magistrates' courts considering petty sessions or adult courts, and we must now turn our attention to magistrates' work in other jurisdictions to enable us to complete our picture of the vast amount of work for which they may be eligible.

Young persons and the youth court

Children and young persons have been treated separately by the courts for over a century. The Children Act 1908 provided a 'children's charter' which allowed them to be dealt with according to their needs, which may be very different from those of adults. Youths courts deal with people during their minority. The age of criminal responsibility below which a person is irrebuttably presumed incapable of crime is ten in this country (raised from eight thirty years or so ago, but still low when compared with other European countries), and so the youngest person liable to be dealt with by magistrates exercising their criminal jurisdiction will be aged ten years. Between that age and their fourteenth birthday, they are known as children, and from their fourteenth to their eighteenth birthdays they are 'young persons'.

A 'child', as defined, is 'rebuttably presumed incapable of crime' and this means that in order to secure a finding of guilt against a child, the prosecution must prove to the court's satisfaction not only that the defendant did the act with the necessary intent, but that in doing so he or she knew that what they were doing was 'seriously wrong'. This means what it says, and the best way of proving it is not circumstantially (although there may be instances where this will suffice) but by a direct question asked of the child by the interviewing officer. The words must be given their natural meaning. It is not sufficient for the Crown to show that the child knew that he or she was merely 'naughty' or 'mischievous'.

Many of the provisions regulating the manner in which youths are dealt with by the courts are contained in the Children and Young Persons Act 1933 ('the 1933 Act'), as amended. Perhaps the flavour of that Act and subsequent ones is captured in s. 44, which provides:

> Every court in dealing with a child or young person who is brought before it, either as an offender or otherwise, shall have regard to the welfare of the child or young person and shall in a proper case take steps for removing him from undesirable surroundings and for securing that proper provision is made for his education and training.

Much water has passed under the bridge, and many changes in society have taken place since those words were enacted, but they have never been repealed, and they continue to provide something of an ideal towards which all magistrates dealing with young persons should strive.

Relationship between the adult court and youth court

It would be very simple if all criminal matters involving persons under 18 were dealt with in the youth court, but obviously a moment's reflection will show that that is impossible. What happens when a crime is alleged to have been committed jointly by an 18-year-old (an adult) and a 17-year-old (a young person)? What happens if a young person is alleged to have committed an offence of a serious nature such as murder, rape or robbery where it is obvious that magistrates' courts powers, whether exercised in the adult court or in the youth court, would be wholly inadequate? Fortunately, statute has intervened to deal with those problems and others, such as the basic one of what should happen when a person is 17 when proceedings are commenced, but reaches the age of 18 at some point before the proceedings have been concluded.

Some of these issues are solved by reference to the Magistrates' Courts Act 1980, which in s. 24 regulates the circumstances in which young people can be dealt with by the Crown Court rather than summarily. It provides that a person under 18 charged with homicide is to be dealt with at the Crown Court, but for all other offences is to be dealt with summarily, save in these circumstances: (a) he or she is a young person and the offence is such as is mentioned in s. 53(2) of the 1933 Act and the court considers that, if the young person is found guilty, it ought to be possible to sentence him or her in pursuance of that subsection; or (b) he or she is charged jointly with a person who has attained 18 and the court considers it necessary in the interests of justice to commit them both for trial.

Clause (a) of that provision needs further explanation. Section 53(2) provides a mechanism whereby grave crimes alleged against young persons can be dealt with at the Crown Court. For it to operate, a young person must be charged with an offence punishable in the case of an adult with imprisonment for 14 years or more, not being an offence the sentence for which is fixed by law, and the court must be of the opinion that none of the other ways in which the case may legally be dealt with is suitable. The magistrates must have regard to the maximum sentence the Crown Court could impose, which is the maximum provided by Parliament for the offence or a term of two years' detention in a young offender institution, whichever is the less. It can be seen that before the magistrates use their powers under s. 53(2) a number of restrictions have to be overcome, and it is only for 'grave crimes' within these criteria that the power should be exercised. The legal advisor will be able to give advice from guideline cases to assist the court to make that judgment.

That deals with the assignment of cases between the Crown Court and the magistrates' courts, but what about assignment between the adult court and the youth court?

The general rule is that charges against persons who have not attained their eighteenth birthdays are to be heard in the youth court, but there are exceptions where an adult and a young person are charged jointly with an offence, or an adult is charged with aiding, abetting etc. the young person in the commission of an offence. Problems may arise where, in a joint charge, the adult consents to be tried summarily and pleads guilty, and the young person pleads not guilty. Where should the trial of the young person take place? The magistrates have a discretion in these circumstances. They can either direct trial before the adult court, or direct that the young person be remitted for trial to the youth court. Before making a decision, the court will listen to representations made on behalf of the parties.

If a young person has pleaded guilty or been found guilty after trial in the adult court, then he or she must be remitted for sentence to the youth court, unless the adult court is satisfied it can deal with the case by way of an order binding over the person (or his or her parent/guardian), or by imposing a fine, or by an absolute or conditional discharge. The court to which the young person will be remitted will be the youth court for the area in which the young person habitually resides.

The other jurisdictional issue between the adult court and the youth court concerns the young person who attains majority at some point after the proceedings have been instituted. There has been much litigation over the years on a number of aspects of this seemingly trivial point, much of it concerned with the right of an individual to elect trial at the Crown Court, which is available as a right only for those of 18 years and over. The key date is the date on which the defendant appears at court for the mode of trial decision to be made. But in the youth court there is no mode of trial decision as such, and the relevant date will be the date on which the charge is put. If on that date, the defendant has attained the age of 18, he or she will have a right to be tried by jury, and the matter should be heard at the adult court. If the defendant has not attained majority on that date, then he or she will be treated as a young person and the youth court will go on to deal with the case even if the accused becomes 18 before the trial takes place. If he or she is convicted, the court will proceed to sentence in accordance with the powers of the youth court.

Occasionally the youth court may have to deal with an itinerant child, without parent or guardian, for whom there is no verification of age. In those circumstances, the court may make a determination as to how old the individual is, by considering height, size, understanding etc., and if satisfied that he or she is a young person can proceed to conclude the case even if information later becomes available showing that the person was, in fact, an adult. This may happen where a birth certificate is produced at a subsequent hearing apparently proving that he or she is an adult.

A defendant who has been given a conditional discharge in the youth court, but who breaches it after attaining the age of 18, should be dealt with by the youth court for the breach, but it is otherwise if a defendant has been given a supervision order in the youth court and after reaching the age of 18 is alleged to have been in breach of its requirements. In those circumstances, he or she will be brought before the adult court.

The youth panel: how is it appointed?

Any young person appearing before the adult court in the circumstances described above appears before a bench of magistrates for that petty sessional division. It may comprise one or more magistrates who are, in fact, members of the youth panel, but that will be a coincidence and not a requirement. The youth court, however, must be staffed with magistrates appointed to the youth panel. There are rules under which youth panel members are appointed and a discrete syllabus for youth panel training. Eligibility for appointment to the youth panel is not especially onerous; the law refers to panels of justices 'specially qualified' for this work. That does not imply formal qualification, but may include those specially interested in the youth of the country whether from professional or social contacts or indeed from bringing up families of their own.

Magistrates are not usually appointed to the youth panel until they have been on the bench for at least a year. Youth panels are elected from the body of the bench every three years. The bench, assisted by some data from the clerk, will wish to know the volume of business that is likely to arise in this jurisdiction, and the numbers who are soon to retire — retirement from the youth panel comes at 65. When numbers have been determined volunteers may be sought, and if needs be a formal election takes place. If the petty sessional division is small, with little youth work, it is possible that one or more neighbouring divisions will form a joint panel. This will enable persons appointed to gain experience at courts within the area of the panel. One of the important features of youth (and indeed family and licensing work) is that one needs to do it fairly regularly to gain and maintain expertise, always remembering that there is the normal adult court work to do as well.

Members of the panel should meet at least twice a year to discuss matters of interest with regard to their work, and after the 'business' part of their meeting is over, they may well have a speaker who may lead a discussion on a particular aspect of youth work or youth sentencing. The purpose of this arrangement is to stimulate interest and expertise. As soon as practicable after the bench meeting has selected members for the youth panel, the panel will meet to elect a chairman, and sufficient numbers of deputies as will enable — so far as possible — each youth court to sit with the chairman or a deputy.

Each sitting of a youth court must include a man and a woman as far as possible, but there are saving provisions for emergencies. Training will take place, and the scheme broadly mirrors the training pattern for a newly appointed magistrate. It can conveniently be divided into three parts: foundation, basic and refresher. Foundation training has as its aim the need to introduce the magistrate to the profile of young offenders, the work of the court and the involvement of other agencies. It consists of observations; information, explanation and discussion on important aspects of the youth court work; and further observation and discussion. This foundation programme must be completed before the new youth panel justice starts to sit.

The basic programme comprises visits to establishments dealing with young offenders, such as an attendance centre and a young offender institution, and explanation and demonstration through practical examples of certain common procedures used in the youth court. This second part of the basic programme is not normally commenced until at least six months after the magistrate's appointment to the youth court panel, and is to be completed within 12 months of such appointment.

Refresher training is what its name implies and must be undertaken by each member of the youth court panel during each three year term of the panel. It is divided into a procedural review, and update of the role of other agencies, and further visits to establishments dealing with young offenders. If this training is conducted imaginatively, drawing fully on the expertise of the relevant agencies, the youth panel magistrate should prove competent to discharge these important duties.

As has been seen above, although the usual retiring age for magistrates is 70, a youth panel magistrate must stand down at 65. Perhaps more than any other, it is useful for younger magistrates to be appointed to the youth panel; indeed a person of 50 or above who has not previously sat on the youth panel is usually deemed unsuitable for appointment. The philosophy underlying this may be dubious, but it does give younger magistrates the opportunity to specialise in dealing with this particular age group. Different arrangements apply for the appointment of magistrates to deal with youth court work in the Inner London area.

There can be no doubt that the youth court remains a jurisdiction of great interest and importance, despite the fact that some of the ethos behind the creation of separate courts for young people has become less important with the passage of time. One of the main reasons for this separate summary jurisdiction was to mitigate the rigours of the adult courts as they then existed, and, as we have seen, to provide a welfare basis for the treatment of the young. Youth courts were to be kept separate from adult sittings to prevent young people from mixing with and being contaminated by adult offenders. In the modern day, we see a pattern of offending by the young which is at its peak between the ages of 15 and 25 years. Many young offenders face charges of crimes of the greatest magnitude in the youth court, and go on to 'graduate' to the adult court at 18 with the relative sophistication of some years of offending behind them. For all that, it is to be welcomed that the welfare ethos of the youth court remains as it did nearly 70 years ago. It must be right that society approaches the young in a way which will place the greatest emphasis on reform and welfare. There are many young people who have had a brush with youth courts and been grateful for the measured and constructive response shown by that court in helping to turn them away from offending towards a law-abiding life. Such individuals are seldom mentioned by the media, but social workers and probation officers will attest to their existence. The youth panel performs a type of service which is seldom straightforward and simple, but which nonetheless can bring its own rewards.

Family proceedings and the family panel

Of the changes to the magistrates' jurisdiction over the last 20 years or so, none has been more significant than the reform and revival of the court's family jurisdiction. Domestic courts as they existed before the implementation of the Children Act 1989 provided a poor man's jurisdiction. They did not deal with divorce or issues of property, nor indeed do the present day family proceedings courts, but they essentially made orders requiring payment of maintenance to a spouse, either for her and/or children of the family. These were payments from income. Custody of and access to children could also be determined. Affiliation proceedings dealt with the maintenance by the 'putative father' of illegitimate children, until swept away by the guardianship of minors legislation. All this work took place in separate courtrooms from those dealing with criminal work, but the aura or atmosphere remained adversarial in character. After all, the next courtroom along the corridor might be hearing a robbery committal.

Since the Children Act, there are still no dedicated family courts, but the magistrates' family proceedings courts now take their place in a unified system of courts dealing with family matters. As well as the family proceedings court, this includes county courts and the Family Division of the High Court. Proceedings can be allocated between the component courts in accordance with subject matter, length and complexity, with a view to the parties being able to have their dispute litigated in a court providing the appropriate level of expertise. Although family proceedings courts are fundamentally unsuited for determining property issues, which may have a complex legal foundation, their local base as part of magistrates' courts sitting in towns and cities throughout the country make them a suitable forum for dealing with emergency applications and a range of public and private law disputes. Much has also been done to separate the work of these courts from other magistrates' courts business. Many magistrates' courts sit in new buildings, some of which have not only a separate entrance for parties in family proceedings cases, but also in some cases a separate suite of rooms in which parties can wait or in which important discussions can take place. Obviously many of these changes have cost money, but virtually everywhere it has been possible to introduce improvements so that attending the family proceedings court is not seen as an ordeal. Much has been achieved within existing court budgets.

Public law or private law

'Public law' in this context means proceedings brought by a local authority, or possibly the police, in connection with the protection of children. One of the disturbing aspects of modern day living is the number of children who are at risk of significant harm through one or more of a number of types of abuse, including neglect. Until the implementation of the Children Act, care cases were dealt with by the youth court (or juvenile court, as it was then called) and this meant that a care case might take its place in a mixed list where there might be a number of criminal proceedings. In short, the juvenile court was a wholly unsatisfactory forum for it.

Now, in the family proceedings court, care proceedings are heard in a list of family matters. Applications for emergency protection orders are also heard by family panel magistrates. This is the mechanism under which a court (or single magistrate) can authorise a social worker or police officer to take a child into protection where the court has reasonable grounds for believing that there is significant harm to the child's welfare or a risk of such harm. This is a quick acting provision which will last initially for a maximum of eight days, although it can be extended for a further seven. The social services department then decides whether care proceedings need to be instituted in relation to the child or, if the situation of the child and the parent/guardian has stabilised, whether the child can safely be returned to the care of that person. Care proceedings are subject to allocation to a different tier of court as we shall see shortly.

'Private law' cases concern disputes between parties themselves, and which do not therefore involve a public element such as the police or social services. These are almost inevitably disputes between husband

and wife or former co-habitants about maintenance or about the residence of and contact with children. Gone (and unlamented) are the days when it was thought that parents had 'rights' to custody or access, almost as if the children were items of property to be fought over. Thanks in large measure to the Children Act, children are seen as *the* important people caught up in what may be a rather depressing saga of disharmony. It is they who have a right to be heard as to with whom they should live and whom they should see, and the court is expected to give weight to their views, provided they are of sufficient age and understanding to express them.

In all decisions affecting children, the court must have regard to the welfare of the child as the 'paramount' consideration. In a disputed case about where a child should live and the contact he or she should have, it is much better that the court supplements the evidence it hears in court about the competing claims of the parties by ordering a welfare report. This will be prepared by a specialist probation officer known as a 'welfare officer', who, over a period of weeks, will conduct investigations between the parties, the child concerned, other family members, and perhaps other agencies, and will then come to a considered recommendation as to what should happen. The court receiving the report is not bound to follow its conclusion, but it must have (and be prepared to articulate) good reasons for not doing so. In many cases the contents of the welfare report will take the heat out of the dispute and the application may no longer be contested, perhaps with some fine tuning of specific issues between the parties. It can be seen that a good welfare report is of inestimable benefit to family proceedings courts.

Reasons

Justices sitting in family proceedings courts must give written reasons for their decisions. It was once the case that magistrates were always advised not to give reasons for any decision, on the rather suspect basis that they may have made the correct decision for the wrong reasons. That is now a thing of the past. Magistrates must be prepared to give reasons in a number of matters in the adult court, for example when refusing, or, in certain cases, when granting, bail; and when they impose any form of custodial sentence in either the adult or youth court. Moreover, in sitting with a judge in the Crown Court hearing an appeal, they must be prepared to give their reasons for granting or dismissing the appeal, though these will be articulated by the judge. But reasons in family cases are as important, and need to be carefully prepared. There is no short cut.

After the evidence has been concluded and speeches made, the bench will retire either with the legal advisor, or the advisor will join the bench fairly soon thereafter. He or she may assist the bench to identify the issues, if these remain unclear, but then it is wholly a matter for the magistrates, and not the magistrates and the legal advisor, to determine what facts have been found on the evidence heard. In other words there is an analysis of what facts are agreed between the parties, what are the facts in dispute, and then what facts the magistrates find proved. There is next a process of making the decision based on the facts agreed and the facts found, followed by specific reasons for that decision. It sounds more complicated than it is. It consists of a structured evaluation of the evidence. The legal advisor will write out the reasons, and there are some very helpful pro formas available. It is a skill that can be honed with practice.

When the reasons have been completed, the bench will return to court and the chariman will read out the reasons. Copies of the reasons will be made available to the parties, who can then consider whether or not to appeal against the decision. Reasons have to be given not only at the final hearing, but also at interlocutory hearings, and this includes decisions made at a preliminary stage when the facts may be unclear. For example, reasons have to be given for the grant (or refusal) of an emergency protection order, but these need not be extensive. They should only cover the evidence which has persuaded the court to make the decision it has, without more, and what aspect of the evidence has persuaded the court that the statutory requirements for the making of an emergency protection order have, or have not, been made out.

Allocation

One of the important considerations in hearing any family proceedings is the question of delay, and the premise that any unjustified delay may be inimical to the welfare of the child concerned. In a legal profession which has traditionally given greater weight to certainty than to speed, that premise, contained in s. 1, Children Act, is much to be welcomed. It also may be a matter bearing on the issue of where the case should be heard, because a backlog in hearing cases in one magistrates' court may be a very good reason to transfer the case to another where delays are shorter. This is simply a question of managing a case so that best use of available resources can be made. As we have seen before, there is no national family court, but those courts which exercise family jurisdiction are 'integrated' as never before. This is shown by the power to allocate proceedings to the appropriate level of court, and the mechanics of doing this are to be found in the Children (Allocation of Proceedings) Order 1991. Proceedings may be transferred from one magistrates' court to another where it is likely significantly to accelerate the determination of the proceedings, or where it would be appropriate for those proceedings to be heard together with other family proceedings pending in the receiving court. The receiving court must consent to the transfer. Those two considerations may also apply to the transfer between a magistrates' court and the county court, but additionally (and importantly) that form of transfer may take place where the proceedings are 'exceptionally grave, important or complex', and the order goes on to give some examples of what is meant by this phrase, for example:

— because of the complicated or conflicting evidence about the risks involved to the child's physical or moral well-being or about other matters relating to the welfare of the child;
— because of the number of parties;
— because of a conflict with the law of another jurisdiction, etc.

Each magistrates' court has a county court to which such proceedings are transferred; in the London area transfer is the Principal Registry of the Family Division.

The same order also deals with transfers downwards from county court to a magistrates' court, and upwards from the county court to the High Court. There arrangements had no equivalent prior to the implementation of the Children Act. Until then the jurisdictional lines were firmly drawn, and it has taken some time for all courts to become accustomed to the new arrangements. By and large, the system works well, although there are sometimes difficulties, for example, a case which may well fall into the 'exceptionally grave, important and complex' category may be transferred up to a court where the delays are such that there are no prospects of a hearing for many months. Nonetheless there is now real flexibility which should go a long way to ensuring that the right level of court hears the case and within an acceptable timescale.

Appointment to family panel

We have seen that youth courts must be staffed by magistrates appointed to the youth panel and presided over — save in the case of an emergency

— by the chairman or a deputy chairman, and a similar provision applies in the case of magistrates' family panels. The life of the panel is three years and the panel is appointed at the annual election meeting of the bench.

Arrangements also exist for the formation of joint panels comprising magistrates from more than one petty sessional division. There is no requirement that a magistrate appointed to the panel be 'specially qualified' as is the case with the youth panel. The prospective family panel magistrate must have been a justice for a minimum of one year, and have indicated that he or she is willing to serve. Temporary transfer may take place from one family panel to another where it will assist the administration of justice. Arrangements for the election of chairman and deputy chairmen to the family panel are similar to those for the youth panel, and the family panel must meet as often as necessary but not less than twice a year, inter alia, 'to discuss questions connected with the work of those courts'. Family proceedings courts should be chaired either by a stipendiary magistrate, who is *ex officio* a member of the panel, the chairman or a deputy chairman, although in an emergency another member of the court may preside.

Different arrangements apply in the Inner London area.

All magistrates appointed to the family panel must receive training before they sit and this continues after they have started to sit. If they aspire to take the chair, there will be further training, and although the burden may appear to be heavy, it is necessary. Sitting in family proceedings courts requires particular skills and insights which are not found in other magisterial duties. The initial training comprises a foundation course of 12 hours' duration which must be completed before a new member of the panel starts to sit. It will cover such matters as the key principles of the Children Act, knowledge of the powers available to deal with financial claims and domestic violence, and an appreciation of the role of different parties, agencies and officers in family proceedings, such as the local authority, guardian ad litem, and welfare officer. The basic programme must be completed between six and eighteen months after the family panel justice first begins to sit. It is of eight hours' duration, and will deal with a number of topics in depth, such as the nature of attachment and the effect of separation and divorce on children, and information on the signs of emotional, physical and sexual abuse. Refresher training consists of 12 hours of training to be completed each subsequent three years, and may include items to consolidate and expand the magistrate's knowledge, such as multi-disciplinary training and a structured self study programme. There is an additional training commitment for those elected to chair the family proceedings court.

Rewards and burdens

It must not be forgotten that appointment to the youth or family proceedings panel heralds a considerable extra burden in training. It is additional work, although most panel magistrates could rightly expect some diminution of their petty sessions sittings. It is likely, however, that magistrates will seldom be able to sit in petty sessions and in the youth and the family proceedings courts: the burden would be too great. Although there is no legal impediment to a magistrate serving on both panels, the Lord Chancellor disapproves of magistrates sitting on both panels at the same time, and many benches are adopting an informal rule that a magistrate wishing to serve on one of the panels will be appointed either to the youth panel or to the family proceedings panel, but not to both. It is suggested that there is some merit in such arrangements. After serving two or three terms on one panel, the magistrate may seek appointment to the other, thus rounding his or her experience.

Liquor licensing and betting and gaming licensing

We have examined the system of 'panels' which recognises the importance of a degree of specialisation on the bench and provides the opportunity to develop experience in a particular area of work. Licensing is in some respects the same, and in others different. The licensing of liquor establishments is an example of the administrative jurisdiction of magistrates which was such a large part of their work until the creation of local authorities in the nineteenth century. Magistrates were until then responsible for the maintenance of highways and bridges, among other responsibilities which are now performed by local councils. Most of this administrative work has been swept away, and magistrates are left with pubs, clubs, bookmakers' permits, betting office licences, bingo hall and casino licensing and certain types of gaming by machines. The control of the old 'music and dancing licence' which regulated musical and other entertainments of a public nature has now passed to local authorities, and periodically it is suggested that the rump of the administrative jurisdiction should follow.

However, although an impartial observer might say that this jurisdiction is a 'rag-bag' of administrative work, this residue is an important area of jurisdiction, and evidence suggests that magistrates discharging these duties take great care over them.

Liquor licensing

Although certain licensing matters, such as the grant of protection orders, occasional licences and club registration certificates, fall within the province of the magistrates sitting in petty sessions courts, the bulk of the work is done by the licensing committee sitting as a committee in the court building. The committee will hold a general annual licensing meeting ('brewster sessions') at which licences may be granted or transferred, amusements with prizes permits issued, and occasional permissions considered. It will also hold a number of other meetings conveniently spaced throughout the year at which this business can be conducted. The licensing committee is elected every year at the annual election meeting of the bench. It has between five and twenty members, and the committee elects a chairman, who is expected to preside when available, but the committee may sit in divisions, so that two committees may sit simultaneously if the amount of business justifies a division.

The licensing committee will sit in a courtroom and its hearings are open to the public. How is it distinguishable from a court? It is stressed that it is a body discharging *administrative* functions, but it must act judicially, for example, by not prejudging an application and by agreeing to hear all sides such as the applicant and his or her witnesses and any objectors there may be. The committee must act fairly and justly and not according to whim or against the weight of the evidence. However, the great merit of a licensing committee as opposed to a licensing court is that it may formulate policy as it thinks fit as to the discharge of different aspects of its responsibilities. It may also formulate notes of guidance for applicants so they may know the committee's view about the use of plans, petitions and the like. Local knowledge of the area of the committee will be essential in constructing a policy. If the area has been flooded with off-licences, the committee may decide to make as part of its policy a minute that:

> although every application for an off-licence will be carefully considered, it is the policy of the committee not to grant a new off-licence to any part of the division which appears to be adequately served.

A policy document may address any number of similar matters, but two things must be remembered, first that the policy must be published, it cannot remain a secret document for the benefit of the committee to consider behind closed doors. Secondly, that each application for an off-licence must be carefully considered and an application must not be prejudged in line with the minute of policy. In most divisions, there have been examples of an applicant being able to show that the application falls outside the terms of the policy or that the application is, for example, of such a specialised nature as to fall outside the concerns that the committee had in mind when the policy was formulated.

Decisions made by the licensing committee are subject to appeal. In most cases this is to the Crown Court where the appeal will be heard by a judge and four magistrates. Two will be from the licensing committee whose decision is being appealed against (although obviously they will not have been members of the actual committee that made the decision) and two magistrates from other licensing committees.

Betting and gaming

The betting and gaming licensing committees are in law separate entities from those dealing with liquor. In some divisions, the same magistrates are appointed, although this is obviously not a requirement. The betting committee deals with applications for the grant or renewal of book-makers' permits and betting office licences; the gaming committee deals with applications for bingo club licences and, in certain areas of the country, casino licences. Rights of appeal are to the Crown Court. The work of these committees should not be underestimated. Grants or refusals of the sort of application that is heard in these committees may have a substantial effect on the amenity of the licensing area, and in some respects it can be high profile work. Many nationally known companies may be behind the applications, and the quality of preparation and advocacy before these committees may be of a very high order.

Training

It has been seen that the election of magistrates to the licensing and betting and gaming licensing committees takes place at the bench's annual meeting held in October. The odd feature, when compared with the other special jurisdictions of the youth panel and the family proceedings panel, is that there is no obligatory training before or after appointment. This is a pity and should be remedied. The importance of this work, and the skill required to discharge it, may be considerable, particularly in large urban areas. Indeed, for those divisions where the committee has a policy to carry out periodic inspection visits to each of the licensed premises in the division, it can be demanding as well as time consuming. But although training is not obligatory, it does not mean that none is carried out. Many licensing committees carry on in practice as if they were akin to one of the other specialist panels; they have meetings where not only different aspects of their jurisdiction may be discussed and training performed, but there may be opportunities to invite speakers to deal with topics of particular interest. Despite the strange lacuna in compulsory training, there is every indication that licensing committee magistrates are as committed to their duties, and knowledgeable about them, as those following other specialisms.

Conclusion

This chapter proves that a general perception that magistrates spend their sittings dealing with minor thefts, assaults and speeding cases is a gross over-simplification. Much of the important work of the bench consists of specialist matters, and magistrates will develop particular interests and skills in tackling these duties. In different ways, the informed decisions taken in balancing competing arguments as to whether a baby should be made the subject of a care order or whether the gaming committee should grant a licence for a proposed bingo hall in the teeth of local opposition, show not only the diversity but also the importance of work in the specialist jurisdictions open to magistrates.

Eight

Bail in Criminal Proceedings

Introduction

The decision whether or not a court in criminal proceedings should grant bail, and if so whether with or without conditions, is one of the more difficult decisions faced by magistrates and regularly causes concern. The reason is plain: most decisions taken by courts are in respect of events that have actually happened in the past. A defendant has pleaded guilty to an offence of theft from a shop and is sentenced for that offence, for something that he or she has accepted actually happened. Again, a court hears evidence in a contested case and makes findings of fact in determining whether the prosecution has proved the defendant's guilt. The court bases its decision on what it finds actually happened in the past.

The bail decision, however, is not about what happened in the past but what might happen in the future, although what has happened in the past may be a helpful factor in the court's judicial 'crystal ball gazing'. In deciding whether or not to grant bail, a court may be assisted in predicting whether the defendant is a good bail risk by considering whether he or she has previously failed to surrender to bail or whether he or she has committed an offence while on bail. As the court has to make a bail decision, for the most part, only when a case is adjourned, the fewer adjournments that are granted, the fewer bail decisions have to be made. It is axiomatic that a court must carefully consider all applications to grant adjournments — even so-called 'agreed adjournments' between the parties — and grant such an application only where it is just to do so. It is then that the bail decision comes into play.

The Bail Act 1976

The Bail Act 1976 (as amended) provides the framework for the bail decision. It creates a statutory right or presumption in favour of bail for any person who is accused of an offence, when he or she:

— is before a magistrates' court or the Crown Court in connection with the offence; or
— applies to a court for bail in connection with the proceedings.

It also applies to a person who has been convicted of an offence and whose case is adjourned for enquiries or a report to be made to assist the court in dealing with that person for the offence. It extends to a person who has been convicted and sentenced, but is back before the court accused of breach of the requirements of a probation, community service, combination, or curfew order.

Insufficient information to make bail decision

The general right in favour of bail exists unless it is excluded by operation of the Act, but before we examine the circumstances in which bail may be withheld, and a defendant remanded in custody, there is a helpful provision which deals with the common situation where a court feels it has inadequate information to make a bail decision. There may be serious doubts about a person's identity or address and community ties, or perhaps a check on his or her criminal history is awaited. The defendant need not be granted bail if the court is satisfied that, owing to lack of time since the commencement of the proceedings, it has not been practicable to obtain sufficient information to take the decision required. The court may therefore remand in custody for a period to enable these matters to be resolved. Although a court may sometimes be justified in remanding for the full eight clear days, this will be rare. Often the information needed will be made available in a day or two, and the court should remand for the shortest period necessary so that the interests of the defendant can be protected by a full bail application as soon as practicable. This power is a useful one, but it must not be abused. As in all decisions involving bail, the liberty of the subject is the central issue, and in most cases the defendant is unconvicted.

Power to withhold bail: imprisonable offences

There are a number of grounds, listed in sch. 1 of the Act, on which a court may withhold bail. The three most important are that a defendant need not be granted bail if the court is satisfied that there are substantial grounds for believing that the defendant, if released on bail (whether subject to conditions or not) would:

— fail to surrender to custody; or
— commit an offence while on bail; or
— interfere with witnesses or otherwise obstruct the course of justice, whether in relation to himself or any other person.

It can be seen from the outset that a high degree of certainty is required before bail can be withheld. 'Substantial grounds' needs no further definition, but means precisely what it says. If, for example, some grounds exist but they are not 'substantial' then bail must be granted, although it may be appropriate for that bail to be conditional. It is not a ground for withholding bail that the defendant faces a serious charge, or has a bad criminal record. Persons facing serious charges are regularly bailed and answer to their bail in accordance with the law, and persons with bad criminal records often manage to survive their bail periods without offending.

In applying the test described above, the court must have regard to a number of non-exclusive factors. These may seem fairly obvious, but it is helpful that they are included in the Act because it enables courts to approach any bail decision in a structured way. The factors to be considered are:

— the nature and seriousness of the offence and the probable method of dealing with the offender for it;
— the character, antecedents, associations, and community ties of the accused;
— his record of answering bail in the past;
— the strength of the evidence against him.

Consideration of these factors may mean that a defendant with a substantial criminal record, but who has always surrendered in the past and who has never committed an offence on bail may not have the presumption in favour of bail displaced. The last factor in the list may be troublesome because at an early remand hearing the evidence may still be being collated. In some cases forensic analysis of items seized will not be available and may not be so for many weeks. Or perhaps the case depends entirely on identification evidence which cannot be tested before the trial or, conceivably, committal proceedings, again some time in the future. But then there is the situation where a defendant is caught red-handed committing the crime, and the evidence is overwhelming. Strength of evidence is only one factor, however, and the court will be required to perform a balancing exercise in determining whether the strong presumption in favour of bail has been displaced. Other exceptions to the presumption in favour of bail include where:

— the defendant has previously been released on bail in the same proceedings and has been arrested for absconding whilst on bail or breaking the conditions of bail;
— the court is satisfied that the defendant should be kept in custody for his own protection, or if he is a child or young person, for his own welfare;
— the defendant is in custody in pursuance of a sentence of a court.

Power to withhold bail: non-imprisonable offences

The grounds on which bail may be withheld in the case of non-imprisonable offences are much more limited. They include the three circumstances listed immediately above, with one additional exception to the presumption in favour of bail. The defendant need not be granted bail if:

— he has previously failed to answer bail; *and*
— the court believes that if released he would fail to surrender to custody.

Conditional bail

In the lead-in to the enactment of the Bail Act 1976, it was widely thought that a defendant appearing before the court for whom the presumption in favour of bail existed would be dealt with in one of two ways. If the court were satisfied that a substantial ground or grounds existed for withholding bail, then the defendant would be remanded in custody, but if not, would be granted unconditional bail. The power to impose conditions on bail existed in the Bail Act from the beginning, but the architects of the legislation would surely be surprised at the frequency of conditional bail, and the tendency of courts to use conditional bail as a 'halfway house' between withholding bail on the one hand, and granting unconditional bail on the other.

Before imposing conditions, a court must find that unconditional bail is inappropriate but that there are no substantial grounds which would justify withholding bail altogether. Conditions have to be imposed for good reason, and not on mere whim. In a decision arising from the 1984 miners' strike, Lane LCJ held in *R* v *Mansfield JJ, ex parte Sharkey* [1985] QB 613, that conditions could be imposed to meet a real (rather than a fanciful) risk, and they must be imposed to help meet one of the three grounds listed on page 123. This means that if a court finds no substantial grounds for withholding bail on the basis that the defendant would abscond, yet it is satisfied that there is a real risk that he or she might, conditions designed to meet the risk may be imposed on the defendant's bail. Thus the taking of a surety before granting bail, together with a condition of residence once released on bail, may be appropriate.

There is a danger that a defendant's bail may be overloaded with conditions, and magistrates must remember that any condition imposed restricts the liberty of a defendant. Only the minimum necessary conditions should be imposed. As a useful rule of thumb, magistrates considering the imposition of conditions should remember the three Es: conditions should be exact, efficient, and enforceable. A condition, for example, 'not to enter the Wembley area' fails the first of these tests; it is inexact in that it does not represent a precise geographical area. The same criticism can be levelled at a condition, 'not to contact prosecution witnesses' unless the names of the witnesses are specified precisely so that the meaning of the condition is clear not only to the defendant, but also to the police. A condition of 'reporting to X police station each Saturday at 8 pm' is almost certainly ineffective to meet the risk of a defendant absconding. A defendant could report within the terms of the condition this Saturday, and be at the other side of the world well before next Saturday. The idea that reporting will enable the police 'to keep an eye on the defendant' is largely whimsy! The imposition of a surety in an appropriate amount may be a better bet, and if there are real fears that the defendant will leave the jurisdiction, the deposit of a security (i.e., a cash sum lodged with, or to the order of, the court), and the surrender of the defendant's passport to the police with a prohibition against applying for any passport or travel document, may fit the bill.

Absconding

The Bail Act, s. 6 creates an offence of absconding when on bail. This may take one of two forms. The more common is where a person released on bail fails without reasonable cause to surrender to custody. The burden of showing reasonable cause lies on the defendant, and the standard of proof will therefore be on the balance of probabilities. The second offence of absconding is where a person has been bailed to surrender on the due date and has a reasonable cause for not surrendering on that date, then fails to surrender as soon after the appointed time as is reasonably practicable. Both these offences carry the same maximum penalty: on summary conviction, imprisonment for up to three months and/or a fine of £5,000; or by the Crown Court as a criminal contempt of court by up to twelve months' imprisonment and/or an unlimited fine.

The cause for failing to surrender must be 'reasonable' and courts regularly have to examine reasons for non-appearance to see whether they provide a defence to the offence. Illness which is certificated is a common cause, although doctors' certificates or notes should be carefully scrutinised for it does not necessarily follow that a defendant who is unfit for work is unfit to attend court. Defendants who have mislaid charge sheets, bail forms or other notices, or have simply forgotten the date on which they are due to surrender have, it is submitted, no reasonable cause, although the court will have to consider each case on its own merits.

The commencement of proceedings for absconding depends on whether the defendant was bailed to court by a police officer from a police station, or bailed by a court on a previous occasion. In the former case, the proper procedure is initiated by charging the defendant or, more usually, by laying an information to which the defendant will enter a plea. In the latter case, the defendant has, on the face of it, defied a court order and the court will initiate proceedings of its own motion. The prosecutor nonetheless conducts the proceedings and in a disputed case calls evidence.

The application for bail

It is often assumed that bail is only ever granted after a spirited application by the defendant's advocate, but the Bail Act imposes a duty on the court to approach a bail decision in a way which is quasi-inquisitorial in nature. This means that the court must actively consider whether bail should be withheld, and if so on what grounds, even if there is an indication from the defence that there is no application for bail. Of course, it may be that the grounds for withholding bail advanced by the prosecution can be put before the court much more concisely than if there were a full application, but the court must still make findings as to the legal grounds for withholding bail and give reasons for its decision. On subsequent applications, the Act states that, 'it is the court's duty to consider at each subsequent hearing ... whether he ought to be granted bail'. The general rule governing the hearing of applications for bail must always be viewed in the light of that duty. But a defendant does not have a right to make bail applications on appearance after appearance rehearsing the same points each time without success. Full applications may be made on the defendant's first two appearances before the court. After that the making of an application will depend on the existence of some new factor, whether as to fact or as to law, which the court has not heard previously. The precise wording of the Act needs to be considered:

> At the first hearing after that at which the court decided not to grant the defendant bail he may support an application for bail with any argument as to fact or law that he desires (whether or not he has advanced that argument previously). At subsequent hearings the court need not hear arguments as to fact or law which it has heard previously.

The onus of showing that a further bail application should be allowed lies with the defendant, but in a marginal case it is submitted that the court should always err on the side of hearing an application. Failure to do so may result in the defendant remaining in custody for many weeks. It is submitted that at the stage of committal to the Crown Court a court should carefully review bail, although there is no specific necessity to hear a full bail application again. The reason is that after committal the case passes out of the control of the magistrates' court, and it may mean that many weeks will pass before it will be listed in the Crown Court, although since the advent of plea and directions hearings in the Crown Court a defendant will normally make a first appearance there in between four to six weeks. In addition, where the defence has conceded at committal stage that there is a *prima facie* case (see page 78), the court has the first real opportunity to assess the strength of the evidence against the defendant. Although this will generally be statements in written form only, at least some sort of assessment can be made, and that may lead to the grounds for withholding bail being confirmed or modified.

Any court hearing a bail application must comply with the principle *audi alteram partem*: both sides of the argument must be heard. Typically the Crown will be asked to state its objections or observations about bail. The prosecutor will detail the offence(s) and the circumstances under which the defendant came to be arrested. Details may be sketchy, particularly if the case is a 'first appearance' or an 'overnight'. In other cases the evidence appears strong, but it must be remembered that it is highly exceptional to hear evidence at remand hearings, so the court will have to make what it can of the prosecutor's representations. After detailing the allegations, the prosecutor will put before the court particulars of the defendant, what is known of any community ties and previous criminal record (if any). The prosecution will conclude by giving its views about bail, and if the prosecution feels it should be withheld, the reasons why.

The defence will then apply for bail, perhaps first commenting on the allegation, any apparent weaknesses in the evidence, and so on. Information will then be given to the court on behalf of the defendant. The intention will be to set the magistrates' minds at rest. For example, it may be said that the defendant is a local person with strong community ties who has always answered bail in the past; that despite a criminal record the defendant has never committed an offence while on bail; that despite convictions for violence, the defendant has never approached or interfered with witnesses before previous trials etc.

The defence may concede that if bail were to be granted conditions should be imposed to meet the risks which concern the court, and then to go on to list suitable conditions with which the defendant would be able to comply. The court then makes its decision, applying the tests laid down in the Act. If bail is refused, grounds and reasons must be given. If bail is granted with conditions, the court must state which real (as opposed to notional or vague) fears under the Act the conditions are imposed to meet.

Appeal against the refusal of bail

If bail is withheld from a defendant after a court has heard full argument, the defendant may well wish to consider appealing against that decision. If he or she is unrepresented, the court, on withholding bail, must tell the defendant of the right to appeal to the High Court. In any event when bail is withheld after full argument, the court is obliged to issue a 'full argument certificate', which sets out in writing the grounds on which bail has been withheld and the reasons for applying those grounds. This document is vital to the appeal process, for a certificate will have to be lodged with the High Court or Crown Court before an appeal can be entertained. The appeal is heard by a judge in chambers, and in the absence of the defendant who is not brought from prison or the remand centre for the appeal. The judge, having heard both sides, has a free hand to grant unconditional or conditional bail, or to remand the defendant in custody as the magistrates' court had done, on the same or on other grounds. If bail is granted, the magistrates' court is sent a notice detailing any conditions imposed on the bail.

Reasons for the grant of bail

Although there is no duty for a court to give reasons for granting bail, public concern about instances of persons committing rape whilst on bail for a like offence persuaded Parliament to amend the Bail Act to lay down categories of cases where reasons have to be given.

Where a defendant is charged with murder, manslaughter, rape, attempted murder, or attempted rape, and the prosecution has made representations that the defendant will fail to surrender, commit an offence on bail or interfere with witnesses etc. (see page 123), the court, if it decides to grant bail, must state the reasons for its decision and those reasons must be included in the court record.

The difficulty in what is otherwise a straightforward provision lies in the phrase 'made representations'. It must be noted that it is not necessary for the Crown to have opposed bail to trigger this requirement, merely that it has made comments or expressed concerns about one or more of the three matters. It is a worthwhile exercise for a court to give reasons in all cases where it decides to grant bail to a defendant charged with one of these offences.

Prosecution's right of appeal

The prosecution has a right to appeal against the decision of magistrates to grant bail. It was conferred by the Bail (Amendment) Act 1993, and applies in restricted categories of cases. The offence with which the defendant is charged or of which he or she has been convicted must be punishable in the case of an adult with five years' imprisonment or more, or be an offence of taking a motor vehicle without consent, or aggravated vehicle taking; the prosecution must be conducted by the CPS or other prescribed prosecutor; and the prosecution must have made representations against the granting of bail before it was granted.

Various procedural requirements must be complied with by the prosecution. Oral notice of appeal at the time of the decision must be followed within two hours by a written notice of the decision to grant bail being announced by the court. If no written notice is served at the conclusion of the two hour period, the right of appeal will lapse. Assuming however, that such notice is served, the magistrates are then obliged to remand the defendant in custody pending the determination of the appeal by the Crown Court. This is treated as a matter of urgency, and must be heard within 48 hours, excluding bank holidays and weekends. The appeal at the Crown Court is by way of rehearing, and the judge has a discretion to grant bail, with or without conditions, or to remand the defendant in custody in line with the provisions of the Bail Act.

Structured decision making

Whether the enactment of the Bail Act 1976 has proved to be a success depends on one's viewpoint. There is no doubt that there is a large and rising remand population in the country's prisons, but crime levels have soared since the mid 1970s so it is not appropriate to criticise the practical workings of the Act from that perspective. A positive benefit of the Act has been the requirement for courts to approach the potentially difficult decisions of whether bail should or should not be granted according to a clear, statutory structure. Courts that carefully apply the tests laid down in the Act certainly make better informed decisions, and the risk of injustice is reduced. Relevant issues remain at the forefront, and hunch, whim and suspicion are seen to have no place in the courts' deliberations.

Nine

Sentencing

Introduction

The sentencing of offenders is at the very heart of magistrates' work, and the process by which an offender is sentenced deserves the greatest possible attention. Conventional wisdom in the public house or the bus queue has it that it is a task that should cause few difficulties, but once a magistrate sees at first hand the almost infinite variety of factors that can influence the sentencing decision, it can seem not only problematical but sometimes almost impossible to get right. It is true to say that no two cases are alike. Sentencing is neither an art nor a science, although it may contain elements of both. It is not possible to become an 'expert' in sentencing, although it is perhaps right to say that the more one does it, then the more one feels confident in exercising one's powers, assuming, of course, that the appropriate criteria are applied. The new magistrate should hope to gain a working knowledge of the framework of sentencing, and of the guidance that is readily available, but should always turn to the legal advisor in court for specific advice on the do's and don'ts because of the many pitfalls that exist for the unwary. There is, for example, an extensive volume of guideline cases, and a great many statutes which govern the powers of magistrates' courts in this field.

General principles

The traditional definition of criminal sentencing as the 'lawful punishment of the individual at the instance of the state' is no longer valid as it tells only part of the story. Sentencing does provide lawful authority for punishment, but the sentence of a court in a particular case need not be solely punitive in nature, indeed it need not be punitive at all. Any sentence will give effect to one or more of the general principles of sentencing, and as we shall see a particular sentence may emphasise one principle to the exclusion of the others, or may comprise a mixture of some or all of them. A developing theme has been the function of sentencing as a 'restriction of liberty' not only in the most obvious sense where there is a deprivation of liberty by imprisonment or detention, but also when a community sentence places obligations on an offender which deprive the offender of what would otherwise be free time. The general principles of sentencing are as follows.

Retribution

This means punishment on behalf of the state for wrongdoing. At the top end of the scale, one can immediately think of long periods of custody that may have been imposed for a particular crime or series of crimes, but retribution can also be rather more humble than this. Many of the offences which are regulatory in nature (such as a vast number of road traffic offences) are dealt with by fines, which are nothing more than simple and effective retribution for the offence that has been committed. So the speeding motorist, or the defendant who is fined for obstructing the highway receives a retributive sentence just as the serial killer receives a retributive sentence. Only the scale differs.

General deterrence

This means the passing of a sentence which will deter potential wrongdoers from committing offences. Thus, if there is a spate of offences of criminal damage in telephone kiosks, the court may decide that sentences have to be passed which will deter people who might be tempted to offend in this way. The limitations of this sentencing principle can be seen, at least as far as the magistrates' courts are concerned. Powers of sentencing are much more restricted than in the Crown Court. It may well be that the maximum sentence that could be passed for an offence of this kind is three months, which is hardly likely to deter many potential offenders. Another problem is that general deterrence depends for its efficacy on the sentencing approach being publicised. As few hearings in the magistrates' courts are reported in newspapers or on radio/television, there is no way that the 'message will get home'. It can only be left to the bush telegraph, which can be highly effective but rather erratic in its effect.

Specific deterrence

This means the passing of a sentence which will deter the particular offender in front of the court. This has rather gone out of fashion as an approach since the enactment of provisions in the Criminal Justice Act 1991, giving effect to the 'just deserts' principle, i.e., that one gets one's just deserts as a sentence, no more and no less, although there is power under that Act for courts to pass longer than normal sentences for violent or sexual offences where the court is of the opinion that such a sentence is necessary to protect the public from serious harm from the offender. The suspended sentence of imprisonment, the use of which has markedly declined since the implementation of the 1991 Act, is an example of a sentence of specific deterrence in that if an offender commits another imprisonable offence during the period of suspension, the period of imprisonment which had been suspended will be implemented.

Rehabilitation

This means the passing of a sentence the aim of which is to rehabilitate the offender so that there will be less likelihood of offending in future. The traditional focus of probation has been rehabilitative and this remains the case despite the fact that recent penal policy emphasises the restriction of liberty implicit in an offender attending regularly at the probation offices. But the value of a probation order in rehabilitative terms is pointed up when it is remembered that a number of conditions can be added to deal with, e.g., drug dependency, or hospital treatment for mental illness. The conditions that may attach to an order are infinitely variable, and have an individual focus.

Restriction of liberty

This concept was most usually allied to the imposition of custodial sentences for reasons which do not need further explanation, but the philosophy on which the Criminal Justice Act 1991 rests recognises the fact that community sentences such as probation and community service orders, by the demands placed on those performing them, imply a real restriction of liberty.

Compensation to the victim

One of the developing principles of sentencing is the importance of considering the needs of the victim. Traditionally, the criminal justice process involved the state on the one hand, and the defendant on the other. Offenders, who either pleaded guilty or were convicted, were punished by the courts and that was the end of the matter. It is surely a wholly welcome development that victims, though not formally parties to the proceedings, can claim monetary compensation for the wrong done to them. This may be for an actual loss, such as a sum of money to compensate for the cost of repairs for criminal damage caused, or for money to compensate for, say, the pain and suffering caused as the result of an assault. A court must always consider compensation for the victim, and as we shall see, compensation for the victim takes priority over any other financial imposition ordered by the court. Two important limitations prevent complete satisfaction of the victim's loss. The first is that the magistrates' courts have a limit of £5,000 as to the amount that they can award, and more importantly, before a court can make a compensation order it must have regard to the ability of the offender to pay. As it is generally desirable for financial orders to be paid within a year (or perhaps 18 months at most) it can be seen that an offender in receipt of state benefit is in reality unlikely to be able to pay more than about £250–£300. Compensation is considered in more detail below.

Restitution

The idea of making direct restitution for an offence is a concept in its infancy although there have been various pilot projects in different parts of the country to test the merits of various forms of reparation. It is not every offence that lends itself to direct intervention between offender and victim, and it is not every victim who wishes to listen to an offender's justification for having committed the offence.

The philosophy of sentencing

Since the Second World War there has been increasing Parliamentary intervention in the sentencing framework. Criminal Justice Acts used to come about once every five years, but in the last couple of decades they have appeared with even greater frequency. If one tries to discern a political imperative behind all this activity, it has been to reduce the courts' use of prison because prison places are expensive. There is also a body of research which shows that prison 'does not work'. The best that can be said for prison as a sentence is that for the period that the offender is detained, he or she is not out committing offences. This is an important consideration where the offender is a danger to the public, as in bad cases of violence or burglary, but is a pretty limited goal for many less serious offenders. The depressing feature of penal policy is that the prison population has never been higher; the more attractive feature is that a number of imaginative sentences have been introduced which do not deprive offenders of their liberty by locking them in a prison cell. In other words they are deprived of their free time rather than their liberty. Magistrates, as citizens, know of the publicity given to the prison population and the cost of incarceration, but it is most important that their sentencing decisions are not motivated by cost, or achieving value for money. In accordance with their judicial oath, they must endeavour to do justice according to the law in all cases that are listed before them. Sometimes this will inevitably lead to imposing sentences of imprisonment. Much more often it will enable them to sentence offenders in the community. Of course, it is unrealistic to say that cost should never enter the minds of the court, but it should not be the motivating or deciding factor in passing a sentence.

The present sentencing framework

The Criminal Justice Act 1991 represents a generally successful attempt to provide courts with a workable sentencing framework. It is not perfect. The implementation of the unit fine scheme provided some well publicised anomalies which meant that the scheme had to be withdrawn, soon after it was introduced, by the Criminal Justice Act 1993. Limitations on the ability of courts to consider a defendant's previous convictions were also modified. But those elements apart, the 1991 Act provides a structured approach which has as its aim the need to give offenders their just deserts. The principle of just deserts is long and honourable, and can be traced to Bentham and Austin in our civilisation. The intervention of the courts in terms of sentence must be enough, and no more, than the criminal conduct deserves. Another way of putting it is to say that the sentence must be proportionate to the offending behaviour. This means two things. First, that the court looks at what the offender has actually done. Thus it works from the premise that the offender is sentenced for this offending behaviour, and not for what he or she may have done in the past (because the offender is presumed to have received the just deserts for those previous matters). Secondly, if the conviction is for a number of offences, the totality of the sentences passed must be proportionate to the offending behaviour as a whole. The starting point for the court is, what is the offending behaviour 'worth' in terms of sentence?

The great advantage of the 1991 Act for any court is that it facilitates the idea of a structured approach to sentencing. Whim and prejudice, to which every human being is prone, are minimised if the structure laid down in the Act is followed. In simple terms, it requires that the first consideration is the *offence* which has been committed. The court will look at what the offender has actually done, and then ask itself whether there are aggravating features which make it a bad offence of its type, and then look at mitigating features of the offence which make it less serious of its type. Magistrates will ask themselves whether the defendant has previous convictions and whether those convictions (or any of them) make the conduct under consideration worse. They will then look at the mitigating features relating to the *offender* and whether the preliminary 'ranging shot' as to sentence should be altered as a result of such personal mitigation. They will give credit (of up to about one third) for a prompt intimation of a guilty plea.

The court will be assisted in its task by sentencing guidance from the Court of Appeal and the Magistrates' Association, and often by a pre-sentence report prepared by the probation service. The legal advisor will be able to advise at all times on the law, practice and procedure of the court in relation to the sentencing decision. Despite all these sources of help, the sentence when passed is the responsibility of the court alone. It is a foolish bench of magistrates that ignores legal advice on the framework of sentencing, but guideline cases and the guidance given by others is only guidance, and there may be instances when a bench, in order to do justice, feels it should move away from the guidance. A good discipline in that situation is for a court to list its reasons for reaching the disposal it has. Although the issue of giving reasons has to be approached with great care and lucidity of thought, it is of great assistance to all parties for a court to give reasons for reaching its decision. In certain cases, such as the imposition of custodial sentences and in virtually all decisions made in the family proceedings court, the giving of reasons is mandatory. In other cases, it is often desirable, particularly in instances when the sentence may appear unduly severe or unduly lenient without them.

Pre-sentence reports

An important tool in assisting courts to reach an appropriate sentence is the pre-sentence report. A court will need to focus on gathering information to assist it in its task. It may be assumed that the court knows all it needs to about the offence, for either the defendant has pleaded guilty or has been found guilty of the offence or offences in question, but even with a skilled and experienced defence representative there may still be the need for a court to obtain background knowledge about the defendant. Clearly the court itself cannot conduct its own enquiries as it does not have its own executive arm to carry these out, and so it will ask the probation service to investigate and prepare a written report for the court. It is not every offence that demands this — it would, for example, be absurd if the probation service was asked to use its hard pressed resources to advise a court dealing with an offender convicted of speeding — but courts will normally request such a report if a preliminary view of the case indicates that a community sentence, such as probation or community service, or a custodial sentence might be imposed.

It is good practice for a court adjourning a case for reports to give a preliminary indication as to how serious the case appears. For example, it may seem likely that the prospect of custody is a real one, or in the alternative, that the court is really looking at an appropriate community sentence. If, as is often the case, the court has not any firm view in that matter, it should make clear that 'all sentencing options remain open' so that a defendant cannot say that he or she was impliedly promised some form of sentence but in the event is more severely sentenced. A preliminary view is invaluable for the probation service and for the defendant's legal representative as an indication of the court's thinking. The legal advisor will note on the court papers any such remarks from the bench ordering the report and these will be brought to the attention of the sentencing bench, which will often be composed of different magistrates from that which ordered the reports. Since the Criminal Justice Act 1993, it is no longer obligatory for a court to obtain a report in all serious cases but special considerations apply where the offender is a young person, i.e., under 18, and for young offenders a report should be commissioned where the court's preliminary view is that a community penalty or custodial sentence is likely to be imposed. Good practice requires that a bench give serious consideration to ordering a report on *any* offender facing charges where the sentence is likely to be in these categories.

The pre-sentence report is very much the work of its author, a serving probation officer, but the components of the report are laid down as national requirements. A report will therefore consider the offender's background, attitude to the offending behaviour such as the reason for committing the offence and any genuine remorse. It will look at any personal problems of the offender, such as whether the offence is rooted in domestic disharmony or in alcohol, drug, or solvent abuse. It will then go on to provide a brief assessment of the likelihood of further offending. In the final paragraph of the report, the writer usually comes to a conclusion indicating the sentencing option or options which are the most likely to prevent future offending. The report remains offender-orientated and yet a good report will address the harm done to the victim and whether it is capable of compensation. The conclusion reached in the report is in no way binding on the court, although it will often be followed, particularly where the court has a good working relationship with its probation officers, as is the case in the vast number of instances.

Sometimes there is what is described as a 'creative tension' between magistrates and probation officers, but if they each remember their respective roles, the opportunities for misunderstanding will be minimised. In practice, one of the important committees of a magistrates' bench is the probation liaison committee in which magistrates elected to the committee meet on a regular basis with local probation officers to discuss matters of mutual interest. Although such committees do not exist formally in the Crown Court, there are regular opportunities for members of the judiciary to meet probation officers.

The more common sentences available in magistrates' courts

We shall now consider the more common sentences available to magistrates, assuming that the offender in each case is 18 years or over. Many of these sentences apply equally to young persons but there are a number of distinct sentencing options open to those sentencing in the youth court. The magistrates' court does retain some powers of sentencing over young persons who have appeared jointly charged with an adult. The first duty for the court is to remit the offender for sentence to his or her local youth court, but the adult court may proceed to sentence if it feels it can deal with the matter by way of a fine, a discharge, or by an order binding over the offender.

Discharges and no separate penalty

Absolute discharge

This order is an acknowledgement that the defendant has pleaded guilty to, or been found guilty of, an offence and yet the circumstances are such that the court has no need to impose any penalty. It must be remembered that the defendant is still guilty of the offence, however. It is not the same as being found not guilty (or acquitted) of the offence. An absolute discharge places no obligation on the offender.

Conditional discharge

This order discharges the defendant for any period of up to three years on the condition that if he or she commits any offence within the period of the discharge and is brought before the court, then the defendant can be dealt with all over again for the offence for which the conditional discharge was imposed, as well as for the new offence. If the conditional discharge was imposed at another magistrates' court, then the consent of that court will have to be obtained first. The general rule relating to Crown Court orders is that magistrates' courts have no power to deal with them, unless they were imposed at the hearing of an appeal from magistrates when they are regarded as being the magistrates' court's own decision. Where there is no power to deal with a Crown Court order, there is generally power for the magistrates to commit the offender in custody or on bail to the Crown Court to be dealt with, or merely to request the clerk to write to the Crown Court notifying it of the breach.

No separate penalty

It has been noted above that it is important for courts to approach the sentencing of offences with due regard to 'proportionality'. A great many offences may arise from one incident which do not individually aggravate the seriousness of that incident materially. A classic case is where a motorist driving an 'old banger' is stopped by the police. Numerous offences will be preferred under the Construction and Use Regulations to deal with the defects alleged by the police, e.g., dangerous parts, dangerous condition, four defective tyres, defective steering, lights, indicators etc. Defendants in this type of case are often young and impecunious. On pleas being entered, or on convicting the defendant, the court will determine what the conduct is 'worth'. It will then generally impose fines for the more serious matters, and make an order of 'no separate penalty' or, as an alternative, 'absolute discharge' on the remainder. The use of an order of no separate penalty in respect of offences committed on the same occasion has been expressly approved by the Court of Appeal.

Fines

The fine is by far the most commonly used sentence in magistrates' courts. It is sometimes thought that fines may be unlimited but, with the exception of specific statutory provisions (often, though not exclusively, concerned with environmental protection), fines are limited to scale maxima. Thus all common offences which may be tried in these courts will be expressed as punishable on a certain scale between 1 and 5. At the time of writing, Scale 1 is not exceeding £250; Scale 2: £500; Scale 3: £1,000; Scale 4: £2,500, and Scale 5: £5,000. Thus if one considers, e.g., the offence of threatening behaviour under s. 4, Public Order Act 1986, the Act provides for a punishment of six months' imprisonment and/or a fine on Scale 5.

It may be queried why fines running into thousands of pounds are not regularly imposed in court, and the answer lies in the fact that the scales are only a part of the story. The court, in assessing the appropriate amount of the fine, must have regard to a number of factors. As we have seen, if the offender has caused injury, loss or damage to the victim, and an amount to measure that loss etc. has been quantified, then a compensation order must take priority over other financial impositions. But in imposing any fine, the court is required to consider the means of the offender so far as they are known. There used to be an established principle that this would mean that a fine could be reduced to take account of a lack of means, but could not be increased to reflect the means of a more affluent defendant. That position was altered in the Criminal Justice Act 1991, and the ill-starred unit fine scheme was intended to reflect more accurately that part of the offender's income that could be applied towards the payment of a fine. Even though the unit fine scheme has been abolished, the court is still required to assess a just fine in each case, having regard to the offender's ability to pay. Many courts use a form of means questionnaire to assist in this task. Thus, it may be that in a case not involving compensation, a defendant in receipt of benefit may only be able to pay a maximum of £5 a week towards a fine. Working on the assumption that all fines should, if paid as ordered, be cleared within a year it can be seen that the maximum fine in practice is likely to be in the region of £250, well below most of the scale maxima referred to above. When we consider the manner in which financial impositions are enforced, it will be realised that a key aspect of the enforcement process is to ensure that a just and fair fine was imposed at the outset.

Community penalties

Community service

The idea of an offender making compensation to the wider community for criminal behaviour is long-standing and deep-seated. Yet it was not until the Criminal Justice Act 1972 that pilot schemes for community service were set up in four parts of the country. In the rather gloomy world of penal policy, community service has provided a genuinely bright light. Schemes now exist throughout the country, and provided a court is of the opinion that the offence is 'serious enough' for a community sentence and there is work available, then it can make an order of between 40 and 240 hours. There used to be a debate as to whether community service was an alternative to custody or a sentence in its own right, but since the implementation of the 1991 Act it is unarguably a community penalty. Thus if, after an analysis of all relevant factors, the court is of the opinion that the offence is so serious that only a custodial sentence can be imposed, then plainly a community service order cannot be imposed. Suitability of the offender for community service is not a requirement as such, but it is as well that a pre-sentence report addresses that issue in an appropriate case. It would be quite wrong for a court to set up a defendant to fail, if, for example, there were doubts about his or her physical state of health, but a general lack of motivation is no reason for not making such an order. As with all community sentences, the defendant's consent is necessary before the sentence comes into force. The 1972 Act also created a scheme under which community service could be used to deal with fine defaulters, but that provision has never been brought into force.

Probation order

The probation order is a community penalty, with all that implies. Since the 1991 Act it is no longer permissible for a court to make a probation order in the case of a trivial offence when it is of the opinion that the offender 'needs help'. The offence, after account is taken of aggravating and mitigating circumstances, and any personal mitigation there might be, must be 'serious enough' to contemplate the making of a probation order. Such an order, which will require the consent of the offender before it can come into force, may run for any period between six months and three years, and it may be a simple probation order with only general conditions or may be an order with special conditions.

The sentence is perceived as overwhelmingly rehabilitative in nature, but in recent years policy has moved towards it having more 'teeth'. First, the obligation of being on probation, and actually going along to appointments with a probation officer is seen as a restriction of the offender's liberty in that choice as to how to spend that time is taken away. Secondly, the emergence of national standards as to the enforcement of orders has meant that the supervising officer is obliged to bring back to court a person on probation who has, e.g., missed a specified number of appointments without reasonable excuse. Committing an offence whilst on probation no longer constitutes a breach of the order. An order is now breached only when the offender is shown to have broken the requirements of the order, but a court, in assessing the seriousness of a subsequent offence, may well take into consideration the fact that it was committed when the offender was subject to probation and regard that as an aggravating factor.

What is expected from a probation order?

A probation order, without any special conditions, has as its goal the aim that by working with the probation officer on factors that may have led to crime, the offender may be able to change his or her way of life and thus further offending by that offender can be prevented. Persons placed on probation are required to lead an honest and law-abiding life (the word 'industrious' used to appear, but realistically, with high unemployment, particularly among the young, it is no longer apposite). They must report to the probation officer as often as required and allow the probation officer to visit them in their homes. The offender is expected to listen to the advice and guidance that the probation officer will give.

Although a probation order can be made without the court having first received a pre-sentence report, this is rare in practice. A good pre-sentence report, concluding that probation may be an appropriate disposal, will almost certainly identify a number of issues that the report writer feels should be addressed if the court decides to make such an order. In other words the court may have at least a bare outline of a plan of action that will form the basis of probation work with the offender if a probation order is made.

Once the order is made, the court then has a supervisory role, but only in the broadest sense. Application may be made by the supervising probation officer to amend an order, e.g., by inserting a condition; to revoke an order, e.g., on the grounds of good progress, or where the offender may have received a custodial sentence in other proceedings and thus the order has become unworkable; or to deal with a breach of the requirements of an order. What a court cannot do having made the order is to interfere with the running of the order. It has then become the professional responsibility of the probation service and, subject to the instances just noted, the role of the court has ceased.

A probation order may have one or more special conditions, and again the need for such conditions will almost certainly have been identified in the pre-sentence report. It may be that an offender has committed an offence as a result of frustration against homelessness, and perhaps there will be the scope for a condition that the offender resides during the whole or part of a probation order at an approved probation hostel. It may be that the offending has been to feed an addiction to drink or drugs, and there could be a condition to attend each and every session of a drink or drugs rehabilitation course, which might be residential or non-residential. It may be that the offender is in need of some out-patient psychiatric treatment falling short of that requiring detention under a hospital order; a condition that the out-patient clinic of Dr X at the Y hospital be attended might then be included. There are very many other types of conditions which can be used to cope with particular problems.

It can be seen that the probation order can be a flexible tool which can be adapted to cope with many quite serious cases in the community.

Combination order

The combination order is a community sentence which combines features of a community service order and a probation order. There are limits to the duration of each component. The community service element may be for not less than 40 hours nor more than 100; the probation element may be for not less than 12 months and not more than three years. Even with these restrictions, it can be seen that a combination order is a particularly demanding sentence which, though available to both magistrates' courts and the Crown Court, is perhaps more widely used in the latter. As with other community penalties, the combination order requires consent by the offender in court as a condition of its imposition, though offenders must know that a wilful refusal to consent to an order which has been tailored to their offending behaviour and properly explained by the court, is likely to result in a custodial sentence. It is hardly surprising that failure to consent is rare.

Imprisonment

Imprisonment is the only custodial sentence for offenders of 21 years and over. Young adult offenders, that is persons who are at least 18 and under 21, can receive a custodial sentence, but that will be detention in a young offenders institution. Imprisonment is the most severe sentence available in the magistrates' court. It can be passed if the court is satisfied that only a custodial sentence can be justified for the offence, and then goes on to give its reasons. The giving of reasons does not imply a lengthy judgment, but it does require the articulation and the recording by the legal advisor, in the court register and on the commitment warrant, of one or more clear findings as to why custody is inevitable.

There is of course a limit to the length of a term of imprisonment that may be imposed. As a general rule, this is a maximum of six months' imprisonment for a single offence, but if the maximum provided by statute for that offence is less, then obviously a term in excess of the maximum may not be imposed. Thus the offence of obstructing a police officer in the execution of the officer's duty carries a maximum of one month's imprisonment, and no term in excess of that can lawfully be imposed. An offence of theft carries a maximum of five years when dealt with on indictment, i.e., in the Crown Court, but a maximum of six months when dealt with summarily, i.e., in the magistrates' court. When two or more offences are sentenced together, if they are both summary or one or more is summary and one is either way, then the maximum remains at six months. If, however, there are at least two either way offences, such as a theft and an obtaining by deception, then the maximum is 12 months.

Under the regime laid down by the 1991 Act, persons sentenced to imprisonment will have to serve only one half of the sentence before being released back into the community, though they may be recalled to prison if they offend during the unserved part of the original custodial term. Moreover, a person who has been remanded in custody prior to sentence will be given credit for the period of time spent on custodial remand. This has the effect that the person sentenced does not get what is given, and it often takes quite a sophisticated series of calculations for the prison authorities to work out the earliest date of release. One matter should be stressed, however. It is not the business of a court to try to compensate for the fact that the defendant will be released soon by increasing the sentence. In a real sense that is not a matter for the court. The defendant is sentenced to the just deserts for the offending behaviour, and if that means almost immediate release then so be it.

Committals for sentence

Where a court has accepted jurisdiction in an either way offence and the defendant has consented to be tried summarily, there may well be circumstances in which the court finds that its maximum sentence (normally six months) is inadequate. This could be for a number of reasons, but perhaps most commonly where the defendant's previous convictions show a pattern of offending of the same type, thus aggravating the instant offence. Another example may be where, on pleading guilty, the defendant asks for a number of other matters to be taken into consideration, again aggravating the criminal conduct. Clearly there has to be a mechanism to deal with that situation, and that is provided by the power in s. 38, Magistrates' Courts Act 1980 to commit for sentence to the Crown Court. This power will not take a defendant by surprise because he or she will have been told during the mode of trial procedure of the powers of the court in this respect.

Once the defendant has been committed for sentence, the power of sentence will be the Crown Court maximum, e.g., affray: three years; theft: five years etc. There is no requirement whatever for the Crown Court to sentence in excess of the magistrates' powers. It may be that the offence is seen in a less serious light, or some telling mitigation may appear which persuades the judge to impose a sentence within the magistrates' powers. That is immaterial. The flexibility granted by the section is important. The defendant may have faced charges for other offences at the same time which were summary only, and could not therefore be committed under s. 38. Generally if those offences are either punishable with imprisonment or carry the power to disqualify, they may be committed to the Crown Court too, but then the sentencing powers of the Crown Court are limited to the magistrates' court maxima.

Deferment of sentence

A comparatively underused power is that enabling courts to defer sentence. This can happen only with the consent of the defendant, and may be for a maximum period of six months. The purpose of deferment is to monitor the defendant's conduct after conviction to see whether the specific aims of deferment have been met. It may be, for example, that the offender has expressed remorse for the criminal damage caused to a neighbour's fence, and that at the date of the court appearance has already started to save money towards the cost of repair. The court may decide to test this goodwill and defer for any period up to the maximum, to enable the offender to save the balance and pay it over. A defendant whose offending has been drug-related may have just started a detoxification and rehabilitation programme which will offer him or her a fresh chance. An initial report from the clinic might speak of good progress. Again, the court may consider deferring sentence for the course to be completed.

The court deferring sentence must first be clear in its own mind what it wishes deferment to achieve. If the court is vague in its aims, or wishes to defer rather than take a difficult sentencing decision, then it would be quite wrong to defer — deferment is not 'putting off the evil day'. If, however, the court has clear aims it must decide how long the deferment should last to allow those aims to be fulfilled. It must then spell out to the offender what those aims are and secure his or her consent to the deferment. The offender is given the date on which to return for sentence. The court should ask its legal advisor to write down the aims and ideally a copy will be given or sent to the offender. Certainly, the court papers should be clearly noted.

At the end of the period, the probation service will prepare a report informing the court of the extent to which the purpose or purposes of deferment have been met. The premise under which deferment works is that if the aims of deferment have been achieved or substantially achieved, the court will impose a less severe sentence than might otherwise have been the case, and so there is a real incentive for the offender to do what was agreed at the time of deferment. If the defendant offends again during the period of deferment, the deferred sentence can be brought forward and dealt with at the same time as the new matter.

Similarly, if at the end of the deferment the aims have not been met, then there is no obligation for the court to treat an offender in the more lenient manner that would have followed a successful deferment. It can be seen that deferment works best in cases where there is a very specific aim or objective in mind, and the success in achieving that can be measured easily. Deferring sentence 'to stay out of trouble' or 'to try to find work' is arguably insufficiently targeted and deferment on such woolly grounds is always to be avoided.

Mentally ill offenders

One of the great problems for all those working in the criminal justice system is the number of offenders who are suffering from one or another form of mental illness. Some offenders who may have behaved apparently irrationally may not be suffering from mental illness at all as defined in the Mental Health Act 1983, but from personality disorders which may not be treatable. The 1983 Act provides for intervention by magistrates' courts in closely defined circumstances. The issue of whether or not a defendant is fit to plead is never a matter for a magistrates' court — that is triable by the Crown Court by seeking a special verdict on the issue from a jury. Although the better view is that magistrates have the power to rule on whether the defendant was insane, these complex issues are usually determined in the Crown Court. The magistrates do have power to remand for an assessment of the state of mental health of a defendant, and the power to make a hospital order. Such an order can be made only where a defendant is convicted (or has been found to have performed the act or omission which, save for the absence of the mental element, constitutes the offence) and two psychiatrists have reported to the court that he or she is suffering from one or more of four conditions: mental illness; psychopathic disorder; severe mental impairment; or mental impairment. The court must also be satisfied that a bed is available in a hospital, or will be available within 28 days of making the order. The court can make a hospital order only if the above conditions are fulfilled and it is of the opinion that, having regard to all the circumstances, the most suitable way of dealing with the offender is by means of an order under the 1983 Act.

Enforcement of magistrates' sentences

It is an unfortunate fact of magisterial life that many court sentences are not complied with. Fines are not paid; community service work is not performed; probation appointments are missed. In respect of each sentence of the court, powers exist for defaulters to be brought back to court so that the court can assess whether there has been a default or breach and decide what to do about it.

As far as fines (and compensation and costs) are concerned, the court will conduct a means enquiry during which the defaulter is examined on oath/affirmation to determine income and expenditure and the court will listen to any reasons advanced for failure to pay as ordered. At the end of the examination, the court can determine: to allow further time for payment on terms; to make an order deducting the amount due from the defaulter's wages or benefit; if satisfied that there has been wilful refusal or culpable neglect to pay, to make an order committing the defaulter to prison for a certain number of days (related to the outstanding balance). Such a term of imprisonment may be immediate, or suspended on terms, e.g., that so much per week is paid. It should be emphasised, however, that imprisonment is a last resort as a method of dealing with defaulters. A court must first consider all other methods of enforcing payment and give reasons for deciding that only imprisonment is appropriate. The High Court has intervened on several occasions to quash magistrates' decisions to impose imprisonment when inadequate reasons have been given for the decision. Although a defaulter may in an appropriate case be imprisoned for, e.g., 28 days, if the money outstanding is paid by the defaulter or on their behalf, the person will be released from custody at once. The 'debt' has then been paid. If it is one of those rare cases where if the defaulter actually serves the term of imprisonment, then the 'debt' is wiped out.

Breach proceedings in respect of the requirements of community service, probation, or combination orders are brought to the magistrates' court even if the order was made in the Crown Court. Where the Crown Court made the order, however, unless the magistrates' court thinks that the matter can be dealt with by, e.g., a fine and a direction that the order should continue, the defendant will be committed back to the Crown Court for that court to decide whether or not the order should be revoked and the offender resentenced. The magistrates' court has no power to revoke a Crown Court order unless it was made by the Crown Court as a result of an appeal from the magistrates' court, when it is considered to be an order of the magistrates' court.

A magistrates' court dealing with a breach will first ascertain whether the offender admits the breach. If not, it will have to be proved. Powers on dealing with a breach include the power to fine, not exceeding £1,000, with a requirement that the order is to continue; and the power to revoke the order and deal with the offender in any manner available to the court on conviction for the offence. If the latter course is adopted, the court must take account of the extent to which the offender has complied with the order, and may assume that, where there has been wilful and persistent failure to comply with the requirements of the order, that the offender has refused to consent to a community sentence. This may therefore justify a decision to imprison an offender in breach of a community sentence.

Appeals against decisions of magistrates

Bearing in mind that magistrates' courts deal with a vast number of criminal cases, and a not inconsiderable number of civil cases at first instance, then it is obvious that there must be a sophisticated and well-established mechanism for dealing with cases where the unsuccessful party chooses to appeal. In fact, there are not vast numbers of appeals from magistrates' decisions, which may mean that parties are broadly satisfied with the way they are dealt with, or at least do not consider it worth going to a higher court. It is important for magistrates to appreciate that the fact that their decisions are appealed against does not imply any sort of slight on their ability. Magistrates (or judges, for that matter) should not worry about appeals against decisions in which they have been concerned.

If the appeal is against conviction, the appeal is normally to the Crown Court and will take the form of a rehearing by a judge (or recorder) sitting with magistrates, though obviously not the magistrates who took part in the decision being appealed against. It follows that the prosecution and defence (or appellant and respondent as they have now become) can call the same or somewhat different evidence from that which was brought in the lower court, and the Crown Court can affirm the decision of the lower court, or allow the appeal.

If the appeal against conviction is dismissed, then the sentence imposed by the magistrates will stand unless the appeal is against both conviction and sentence. If that is the case, the Crown Court will go on to consider the appropriate sentence in the light of the information put before it. Again, sometimes material is put before the Crown Court which was not available below, and the Crown Court is fully entitled to consider all matters put before it in deciding whether or not the appeal against sentence should be allowed. Sometimes the appellant complains only about the sentence and if so the Crown Court merely looks at that aspect. The conviction has not been appealed against, probably because the appellant pleaded guilty or having pleaded guilty concedes that the weight of evidence was against acquittal, and the magistrates' finding of guilty was correct.

Where objection is taken to the manner in which the proceedings were conducted in the magistrates' court, perhaps because it is said that the magistrates showed bias in some way, or refused to hear defence evidence, or because the continuation of the hearing constituted an abuse of process, then the appellant may make an application for judicial review. This is a fast growing form of litigation designed to allow the High Court to keep under review the procedures of subordinate courts and tribunals, and to intervene where there has been a breach of the rules of natural justice. It is important to remember that the relief sought by an application for judicial review is discretionary, and there are instances where, although one or more grounds on the application have succeeded, the High Court has not granted the application, perhaps because it is felt that the applicant has not been prejudiced by the outcome, or where the applicants brought the matter on themselves.

The other method of appeal that deserves mention is an application for a 'case stated'. This route of appeal is not confined to the defence, for anyone aggrieved by the decision of the court, whether Crown Court or magistrates' court, may appeal by requesting the court which made the decision to state a case for the opinion of the High Court. The purpose of this procedure is for the Divisional Court to rule on points of law. The procedure is inappropriate where issues of fact remain in dispute. The party seeking to apply for a case stated makes the request to the clerk of the court which made the decision, identifying the question on which the opinion of the Divisional Court is sought. The magistrates can refuse to state a case if they consider the application 'frivolous', which is narrowly construed. It is still possible, though perhaps applied less often than hitherto, for the court faced with an application for a case stated to require the prospective appellant to enter a recognisance to pursue the appeal diligently. One would have thought that might depend on what the case stated says! The clerk to the justices will prepare a draft of the case after consultation with the adjudicating magistrates. The draft case is then submitted to the parties for their written representations, and the final case is prepared and signed by, or on behalf of, the magistrates. It is then submitted to the Divisional Court which in due course will pronounce on the matter, and indicate whether or not the magistrates came to the correct decision on the point in issue.

All appeals have to be pursued within strict time limits, although there is power for the time limits to be extended in an appropriate case. The normal period for appeal to the Crown Court is 21 days from the date of the decision complained of; similarly an application for the court to state a case must be made within 21 days of the decision complained of.

Amending decisions

Section 142, Magistrates' Courts Act 1980, as amended by the Criminal Appeal Act 1995, enables a magistrates' court to vary its decisions under certain circumstances. Formerly the power in the section had to be exercised within 28 days of the decision in question, but now no time limit is laid down. The essence of the section is that a court may vary or rescind a sentence or other order made by it if it appears in the interests of justice to do so. It includes the power to replace a sentence or order which for any reason appears to be invalid by another which the court has power to make. If a court has convicted a defendant and it subsequently appears to the court that it would be in the interests of justice that the case should be heard again by different justices, the court may so direct. Obviously the court may not exercise the power if an appeal has been determined by the High Court or the Crown Court in respect of any question, conviction, sentence or order arising in the proceedings.

This section provides an expedient and effective method of correcting errors that may have been made by a magistrates' court or, short of error, where information has come to its notice after the hearing to suggest that the decision made may have been unfair in some respect. The potential use of the power is endless. It might cover a situation where a bench was found to have acted in excess of its power to sentence; where it went on to hear a case in the (unexplained) absence of the accused only to receive a medical certificate in the post after the hearing indicating that he or she was too ill to attend; or where a number of driving documents not produced by the defendant at the hearing came to light shortly afterwards. In each of those situations, the court may be persuaded to reopen under s. 142 in order to do justice in the case. It must be noted that the decision to employ the section is one for the court, and there is no right for the defendant to insist that the decision complained of be set aside. There are some instances when it would be appropriate to use the section, and still more when the better course is to appeal to a higher court.

Miscellaneous

In this general work it has not been possible to deal with all the sentences at the disposal of the court. Attendance centre orders, orders for one day's detention, and specific sentences for young persons are outwith the general approach of this chapter, but this overview of the sentencing decision and the range of sentences available should assist a justice in understanding the broad range of powers available, and the circumstances in which they will normally be used.

Ten

Making Decisions

Introduction

At the core of the magistrate's work is the task of making decisions. Did defendant A drive in the way the police said? If so, did that amount to careless driving? If so, what punishment is commensurate with that offence? Is there anything about the defendant which makes it appropriate to reduce that penalty? Is there sufficient evidence against defendant B to justify sending him or her to the Crown Court for trial? If defendant C is released on bail, how sure can we be that C will turn up next time? Whom do we believe — PC Wyman or defendant D who are giving conflicting versions of events? If we try this case at the magistrates' court rather than sending it to the Crown Court, and the defendant is guilty, will our powers of punishment be sufficient?

The standard of proof

First, let us look at what has to be proved; how much evidence is needed to reach a particular decision. This is known as the 'standard of proof'.

The presumption of innocence

In criminal cases it has long been a fundamental principle that a person is innocent until proved guilty — the 'presumption of innocence'. This is viewed by many as an important civil liberty fundamental to our constitutional system. In a 1935 appeal to the House of Lords from a conviction for murder, it was put like this: 'Throughout the web of the English criminal law one golden thread is always to be seen, that it is the duty of the prosecution to prove the prisoner's guilt.'

One consequence is that the guilty may go free; the police may simply not be able to find enough evidence to enable the Crown Prosecution Service to secure a conviction, with the result that no case is brought at all, or the case fails for lack of convincing evidence. On the other hand, the principle operates to protect the innocent; it is for the prosecutor to prove the case, not for the accused to disprove it or to establish innocence. The recent introduction of the power for courts to draw inferences from an accused person's silence — to conclude that a person said nothing in order to conceal the truth — has been widely criticised as an erosion of the presumption of innocence, but has nevertheless passed into law.

In civil cases, likewise, the person bringing the case must convince the court of his or her view of matters, although, as we shall see, the standard is lower in the civil courts.

None of this means that it is necessarily wise for a suspect not to contradict what is said against him. If he was in the pub with Fred at the time of the offence, he would be well advised to say so straight away; if Fred confirms it, that may well be the end of the matter.

'Beyond reasonable doubt'

In a criminal case, the prosecution must, if it is to succeed, prove to the magistrates or to the jury 'beyond reasonable doubt' that the accused committed the offence with which he or she is charged. Lord Sankey, in the appeal case mentioned above, went on to say that:

> If, at the end of and on the whole of the case, there is a reasonable doubt, created by the evidence given by either the prosecution or the prisoner, as to whether the prisoner killed the deceased with a malicious intention, the prosecution has not made out the case and the prisoner is entitled to an acquittal. *No matter what the charge or where the trial*, the principle that the prosecution must prove the guilt of the prisoner is part of the common law of England and no attempt to whittle it down can be entertained. (*emphasis added*)

In another case, in 1947, Lord Denning said of the standard of proof that:

It need not reach certainty, but it must carry a big degree of probability. Proof beyond reasonable doubt does not mean proof beyond a shadow of doubt. The law would fail to protect the community if it admitted fanciful possibilities to deflect the course of justice. If the evidence is so strong against a man as to leave only a remote possibility in his favour, which can be dismissed with the sentence 'Of course it is possible but not in the least probable', the case is proved beyond reasonable doubt, but nothing short of that will suffice.

These explanations come from cases of some antiquity, but they remain relevant, which emphasises how deep-rooted and much respected the principle is.

For example, suppose a young man is accused of being in charge of a car while unfit through drink or drugs. The car belongs to him and he is the usual driver. The police caught up with him after he had parked his car and gone into his house. The bonnet of the car was still warm and the young man did not deny that he had driven it. He was arrested and, while on the way to the police station, tried to jump out of the police car and run away. At the police station he again did not deny he was the driver. But when the case comes to trial, he and three of the friends with whom he had been out partying, said that another of the group had been the driver. Because this was the first time someone else had been said to be the driver, the magistrates may decide to give this story no credibility, taking the view that it is too late and too unconvincing to cast a reasonable doubt on the police evidence, and so decide to convict the accused.

Sometimes, the defendant has to carry the burden of proof if he or she wishes to establish a particular defence. A common example is a person who is said to have been driving without insurance, who must produce a certificate of insurance in order to disprove the case. Clearly, it would be impossible for the police or the Crown Prosecution Service to have the task of contacting all the insurance companies in the country, trying to locate a policy, before being able to bring a case. Another example is in connection with the offence of carrying an offensive weapon in a public place 'without lawful authority or reasonable excuse, the proof whereof shall lie on' the accused. Here the defendant must prove his or her defence, but the test is the lower one, 'on the balance of probabilities', the meaning of which is discussed below. So if a person is found with a machete in his car, and says he was on his way to his mother's house to tidy up her overgrown garden, but neither he nor his mother in fact has a garden, the court may be disinclined to accept the defence. But he may fare better if his mother comes to court and confirms that she did indeed have a very neglected garden, was unable to do anything about it herself, and had arranged for her son to come and tame it.

'On the balance of probabilities'

This second test, 'on the balance of probabilities' applies in civil cases and, as we have seen, to defendants seeking to establish certain defences. It is easier to prove something 'on the balance of probabilities' than 'beyond reasonable doubt'. 'On the balance of probabilities' is often paraphrased as 'more likely than not', which comes from the 1947 case mentioned above, when Lord Denning went on say that proof on the balance of probabilities 'must carry a reasonable degree of probability, but not so high as is required of a criminal case. If the evidence is such that the tribunal can say ''We think it more probable than not'', the burden is discharged; but if the probabilities are equal, it is not.'

Statutory presumptions

The law has also developed certain 'presumptions of law' which modify the normal standards of proof. For instance, the Criminal Justice and Public Order Act 1984 makes it an offence to do something:

    (a)   which intimidates, and is intended to intimidate [another person];

    (b)   knowing or believing that the other person is assisting in the investigation of an offence or is a witness or potential witness or a juror or potential juror in proceedings for an offence; and

    (c)   intending thereby to cause the investigation or the course of justice to be obstructed, perverted or interfered with.

The Act goes on to say that if (a) and (b) are proved by the prosecution, then it is presumed that (c) is also proved unless the defendant can establish otherwise. Lay magistrates can expect the prosecutor or legal advisor to bring to their attention provisions of this nature if they are relevant in a particular case.

Structured decision making

All magistrates are now trained in 'structured decision making'. This is a way of sifting evidence, identifying the relevant and eliminating the irrelevant; defining the issues to be decided and discarding the 'red herrings'; evaluating and weighing what has been said in court; and seeking agreement based on the material issues. It has many advantages, not least that it increases certainty that the decision reached is correct. It can also reduce the potential for disagreement between magistrates in the retiring room; it gives magistrates greater confidence in the decisions they reach, and insights which make future cases easier to deal with; last, but not least, in complicated cases it makes decision making easier and faster.

How a decision is 'structured' for these purposes may vary a little from court to court and between different providers of training, but the essential elements are the same: a step-by-step analysis of the case leading up to the decision. Such structures are also the basis for most 'pro formas' for writing reasons in family cases.

Guilty or not guilty?

The way to decide whether a defendant is guilty or not guilty, according to the structured method, is illustrated below, by reference to a sample case. Suppose X has been summoned for driving without due care and attention. It is said that he drove his red Vauxhall Cavalier into the back of a blue Ford Sierra that had stopped at a pedestrian crossing to let someone cross. The incident occurred at 5.30 pm on a clear, dry, summer day. The driver of the blue Ford says that for a quarter of a mile or so before stopping at the crossing, she had been aware that the red Vauxhall behind her was gaining on her and she thought it was going too fast for the road, which is subject to a 30 m.p.h. speed limit. She saw a pedestrian about to step onto the crossing and stopped to let him cross. The pedestrian had just passed in front of her car when an impact from behind made her car catapult across the crossing and come to a halt the other side, causing extensive damage and distressing the driver. The pedestrian for whom she stopped gives evidence that he too saw the Vauxhall advancing on the blue Ford and thought it was going too fast. He confirms what the driver of the Ford has said about the collision. The defendant enters the witness box; he agrees he was driving the Vauxhall in question and that he did indeed collide with the Ford. He says he lives in the area and knows the road well. He says he was not speeding, but that shortly before the collision, a bee had flown in through the car window; it was buzzing around his head and distracting him; he was trying to flick it away with his hand with the result that he did not see the car waiting at the pedestrian crossing. The court's legal advisor tells the court about a case in which a swarm of bees had entered a driver's car causing such a distraction that the driver could not be found guilty of driving without due care and attention.

The magistrates, taking a structured approach to their decision, would adopt a five-stage procedure something like this:

(i)   What standard of proof is required? Standards of proof have already been discussed above, and in this case the accusation of careless driving must be proved beyond reasonable doubt. If the magistrates are unsure which standard applies, the legal advisor will clarify.

(ii)   What constitutes the offence? What elements must be proved by the prosecution? In our example, it would have to be shown that the accused 'drove a mechanically propelled vehicle on a road or other public place without due care and attention'. A Vauxhall Cavalier is clearly a mechanically propelled vehicle and no one has suggested otherwise, so this question can be disposed of immediately. But if it had been a Sinclair C5, and no one had confirmed during the case that this was indeed a 'mechanically propelled vehicle', it might have been necessary to check with the legal advisor. The incident took place in the High Street, and so the 'road or other public place' requirement is met.

More important will be the question, did the defendant drive 'without due care and attention'? In other words, did the driver fall below the standard of driving of a reasonably prudent and competent driver in the situation in which the driver was placed? This is a question of fact for the magistrates alone, and to answer it, we move on to the next stage in the structure.

(iii)   The next step is to review the evidence. If it has been long and complicated, perhaps given by witnesses who are not very articulate, or who do not speak clearly, magistrates may wish to re-read their notes, comparing them with the notes made by their colleagues and by the legal advisor. The magistrates should identify those parts of the evidence which are unclear, contradictory or confused and about which, therefore, decisions need to be made. The process will also highlight those parts of the evidence which are not in dispute; these may well be taken into account when reaching a decision, but the magistrates do not need to decide which, of two or more versions, they are going to accept. At the end of this stage all members of the bench should be clear about what matters are agreed and what matters are not.

Thus, in the example, the magistrates might come up with two lists:

Agreed facts
— At 5.30 pm on Thursday 6 June 1996 the defendant, driving a red Vauxhall Cavalier, drove into the back of a stationary blue Ford Sierra which was waiting to let someone cross the pedestrian crossing outside Marks and Spencer, High Road, Middlemarch.
— The amount of traffic on the road was average for the time, date and place.
— The weather conditions were good.
— The defendant has lived in the area for a number of years; drives the particular journey every weekday and is thoroughly familiar with the road and the pedestrian crossing.

Disputed facts
— The speed at which the defendant was driving immediately before the impact.
— The reason he ran into the Ford.

The questions to be answered can then be formulated as follows:

— Did a bee enter the defendant's car?
— If not, is there any other explanation for the collision? Was the driver simply going too fast? If not, must the facts speak for themselves, i.e., must the magistrates assume the driver was simply not paying sufficient attention?
— If a bee did enter the car, is this the same thing as a whole swarm of bees?
— If a bee did enter the car, is the way the defendant dealt with it within the standard of the reasonably prudent and competent driver or would that person have slowed down and pulled over?

At this stage it may be possible to eliminate certain matters altogether. Thus, the fact that the driver of the blue Sierra was shaken but unhurt is neither here nor there, for a charge of driving without due care and attention is decided according to the standard of the driving, not the consequences. It would have made no difference if the unfortunate woman had in fact been injured.

(iv)   Having clarified the questions to be answered and the evidence by reference to which they will be answered, the next stage is assessing the evidence — deciding whom to believe and whom not to believe, and how important each piece of evidence is. More ideas on how to do this are given later in this chapter.

In our sample case, when deciding whether or not to believe that a bee flew into the car, the magistrates will note that other witnesses did not see it (although of course, they may well not have done); and that no one said they saw the defendant trying to flick the bee away with his hand as he claimed he had done, although again, this is not conclusive — he could perfectly well have done this without anyone seeing. More significantly, the defendant did not mention the intrusion of the bee to the witnesses after the collision, or when questioned by the police. So the magistrates decide not to believe the bee story. But if they had, they would have had to go on and decide whether a single bee should be considered in the same way as a swarm of bees. They would also have to decide how a prudent and competent driver would react to such a visitor. Should he have tried to get it out of the car while driving along, or slowed down and pulled over? If it was not possible to slow down and pull over, should he have simply put up with the bee buzzing around in the interests of the safety of others? Would a reasonably prudent and competent driver be alarmed by the bee? These may be more difficult to answer, and different people will have different views.

(v)   Finally, the magistrates reach their decision. Having eliminated the bee defence, they have to decide whether or not the defendant measured up to the required standard of driving. The magistrates give some weight to the evidence of the pedestrian who said the defendant was going too fast, but not too much, since he did not have a speed gun in his hand and most people have trouble estimating accurately the speed of a passing car. But what he said was corroborated by the driver of the Ford who said the defendant was advancing on her, and this lends it a little more weight. But that is still not sufficient to establish careless driving beyond reasonable doubt. The magistrates decide instead to let the facts speak for themselves. The defendant drove into the back of a stationary car causing an impact which pushed the car forward a certain distance; in the absence of any acceptable explanation, the magistrates have to conclude that he simply could not have been looking where he was going and/or was going too fast. This is below the required standard. They find him guilty of driving without due care and attention.

Of course, many cases are very much simpler than the example used above, and there is often only a single issue to decide which is instantly recognisable, and it is not always necessary to follow all the steps in the structure. But it is hoped that the above fairly detailed example illustrates how the system works to clarify just what decisions need to be reached, and how a careful review and assessment of the evidence before reaching a final conclusion is likely to lead to more reliable decisions in which the magistrates can have confidence.

Sentencing

The 'structured' approach should likewise be applied to sentencing, which is dealt with in detail in Chapter 9. It is pointed out there that the Criminal Justice Act 1991 in fact sets the scene for a structured approach to sentencing. Thus the justices would tackle a sentencing decision in steps such as:

(i) Looking at the offence in isolation from the offender, first, what penalties are available? The court list or other material in use in the retiring room, or the legal advisor, will provide the answer if the justices do not already know.

(ii) The next step is to examine the seriousness of the offence. How much money was stolen — £5 or £5,000? How violent was the assault — a shove with the hand or a blow to the face with a clenched fist? Mitigating and aggravating factors must be identified and weighed to assess how they affect the assessment of seriousness. The sentencing guidelines published by the Magistrates' Association give many helpful examples of features which may make particular offences more or less serious. For example, the fact that the present offence was committed while the offender was on bail in respect of another offence almost always increases seriousness. On the other hand, something done on an impulse in circumstances which made it easier than usual to commit the offence may reduce seriousness.

Many other matters peculiar to the time or place may come into play. For instance, a widely-publicised special effort by the police to reduce the number of crimes of a particular type in a particular locality may call for a greater element of deterrence in sentencing. Any suggestion that a crime is 'victimless' should probably be treated with caution for there is almost certainly no such thing; the victims of housing benefit fraud are the council tax payers; the victims of DSS fraud are the taxpayers. And again, it may be revealed at the outset that there had been a long and detailed argument during the mode of trial proceedings about whether or not the case was suitable for trial by the magistrates, which will immediately signal to the magistrates that, at least at that time, others concerned in the case thought it at the top of the seriousness scale.

This exercise in assessing seriousness should result in a conclusion that the offence is average for its type; towards the lower end of the scale; close to the top of the scale; or at any one of the many points between.

At this point it should be possible to answer the questions:

— (if the offence is imprisonable) Is this offence so serious that only custody is appropriate?
— Is the offence serious enough for a community penalty?
— Is compensation, a fine, or a discharge (conditional or absolute) suitable?

(iii)   The next step is to think about the individual offender to see if anything about him or her makes the bench want to change its mind about what kind of punishment fits the crime. If the bench has in mind to send the offender to prison or to impose a community penalty, it may at this point decide it needs more information and ask for a pre-sentence report from the probation service. If a report has already been prepared, the magistrates will take careful note of the information provided. Thus, difficult personal circumstances such as illness, bereavement or family breakdown may argue for a lower penalty. So too the fact that an offender admitted the offence at an early stage, although if he or she was caught 'red-handed' this will not necessarily carry quite the same weight. It is now appropriate to allow a discount of one third off the sentence for an offender who pleads guilty at the first opportunity to do so. The court will also consider the effect a particular sentence is likely to have, although the fact that an offender has sole care of small children should not necessarily deter a court from passing a sentence of imprisonment if that is otherwise appropriate. The offender's record is also taken into account, a first offender usually being treated more leniently than a repeat offender.

(iv)   The next stage is to consider the purpose of the sentence. Sentencing objectives are reviewed in detail in Chapter 9, from which readers will gather that rehabilitation as an objective of sentencing is giving way to ideas of restriction of liberty and compensating the victim.

(v) Finally a decision on the actual sentence to be imposed must be made. The bench may be unmoved by what has emerged since they assessed the seriousness of the case, or they may take a different view altogether. Suppose a young man pleads guilty to drink driving, having registered 115 on the Lion Intoximeter. Looking at the offence alone, this is an extremely serious matter for which imprisonment, or at least a community penalty, might well be appropriate. But when the circumstances of the offender are revealed, it transpires that a year ago he was a victim in a tragic road accident which left him mentally impaired; he is undergoing intensive psychiatric treatment and has become wholly dependent on his mother; he has already voluntarily surrendered his driving licence to the Driver and Vehicle Licensing Agency, sold his car and taken steps to ensure he does not have access to any other car. A long civil case for compensation for his injuries is in process. On the occasion when he drove, he was suffering a particularly bad episode of instability. In view of all this, the magistrates may decide that a long period of disqualification alone is the most appropriate way to deal with the case. Since, strictly, disqualification is an order ancillary to a penalty, this would be done by imposing 'no separate penalty' or an absolute or conditional discharge for the offence itself, but making an ancillary order of disqualification.

Fixing the level of the penalty brings in many other considerations. If the offence is so serious that only imprisonment is suitable, how short can the sentence be and could it be suspended? In setting a fine, the offender's financial circumstances must be assessed. If more than one offence is being dealt with, should there be separate penalties? Should they be concurrent or consecutive? Are there any subsidiary matters to deal with such as a costs order; penalty points; disqualification; an order to destroy illegal drugs; compensation and so on. Where a number of offences are being sentenced together, the magistrates may well decide to draw up a careful list and double check that every offence has been dealt with, and that, for instance, the total sum to be paid takes account of the payer's means.

It is now good practice for a court to give reasons if it passes a sentence which is harsher or lighter than usual for the type of offence, and at this final stage the magistrates would also come to an agreement on that. It may be a simple matter of announcing a reduction for a timely guilty plea, or may relate to the particularly difficult social situation of the offender.

Considering the offence separately from the offender

The value of considering the offence and the offender separately can perhaps be illustrated by another example. Suppose a driver admits a drink-driving offence and a reading in breath of 120; he was convicted for drink-driving eighteen months earlier. His counsel, who is articulate and eloquent, explains that his client is a person of some standing in the area where he lives; he has a demanding and lucrative job; he is ashamed and embarrassed about what he has done; yes, he is probably addicted to alcohol, but is about to embark on an intensive rehabilitation course at a private clinic. Not addressing the fact that the offence could lead to a sentence of imprisonment, the advocate goes on to say that his client could not perform community service because his time would be completely taken up by his work and the rehabilitation course; that probation is unnecessary since it would only duplicate the therapy to be given as part of the rehabilitation programme; and argues for a fine.

Distinguishing the offence from the offender, the magistrates recognise the offence as one of the most grave of its kind — certainly one for which a community penalty, and perhaps even imprisonment, would be appropriate. They decline to accept the suggestion that providing one's own therapy is an acceptable substitute for a sentence of the court, and adjourn the case for a pre-sentence report, preferring to wait for the more objective views of the probation service before deciding whether there is anything about the defendant's personal circumstances which should modify the sentence that is normally appropriate to the offence.

The adjournment decision

In deciding whether or not to grant an adjournment, magistrates are wise to bear in mind that their courts are courts of 'summary justice', 'summary' here meaning speedy, but not so speedy that justice is compromised. Matters under the Children Act are now subject to the statutory provision that delay is, on the face of it, prejudicial; in other matters before magistrates it is pretty fair to make much the same assumption, and the magistrates have a responsibility for avoiding delay by not granting adjournments unnecessarily. A defendant awaiting trial is presumed innocent until proved otherwise and it is indeed an injustice to subject a defendant to avoidable delay, regardless of whether he or she is finally acquitted or convicted. The fact that both sides agree to an adjournment should not mean that it is automatically granted.

The structured approach to deciding whether or not to grant a request for an adjournment features the following steps:

— How long ago did the alleged offence take place and how many times has the matter already been before the court? What was to have been done at today's hearing and did all concerned have enough time to prepare for that? The court should ask the legal advisor to read out the history of previous listings, including who has previously applied for adjournments, the reason(s), and whether the purpose of each adjournment was achieved on time.

— Is the defendant on bail or in custody?

— Why is an adjournment being asked for now? Can the concerns of the party requesting it be dealt with without an adjournment? For example, by standing down the case for half an hour so that the defence lawyer can take instructions with a view to dealing with mode of trial? Can the defendant be sent home to pick up his or her driving licence so that sentence can be decided?

— What will happen if the case is not adjourned? Will it have to be dismissed? It may be just to do so if this is the second time the case has been listed for trial and the second time that the prosecution has failed to assemble its witnesses. On the other hand, it is not necessarily just to allow an adjournment on the 'score' basis, i.e., that if one side has already successfully applied for two adjournments during the course of the case, and the other side only one, the latter should be allowed another adjournment to 'equalise the score'.

— What is the justice of the matter? Would anyone be prejudiced by postponing the case? If the case has been listed for trial, are the witnesses present, and how many are there? Can the case proceed without one of the witnesses?

— If an adjournment seems the only fair way forward, how short can it be? And does the court wish the file noted as to what is expected next time?

The bail decision

Chapter 8 is devoted to bail and sets out the statutory right to bail and the circumstances in which it may be withheld. Again, decisions on bail can be expressed in a structured way, beginning with the defendant's automatic right, in almost all cases, to unconditional bail:

— What offence is the defendant charged with and does that offence carry imprisonment?

— Is the defendant already on bail, or in custody? If in custody, is he or she there in respect of the present matter, or some other matter?

— If on bail, was bail granted by the police or by the court?

— If a court has earlier refused bail, is the defendant entitled to apply again? What were the grounds for refusing bail? Are there any new circumstances?

Assuming the application can indeed go ahead:

— Has the defendant ever failed to answer bail? Or broken bail conditions?

— In the case of an imprisonable offence, are there substantial grounds for believing that any of the exceptions to bail apply? This is the crux of the bail decision; the grounds for withholding bail are dealt with in full at pages 123–4.

— Are there any reasons for imposing conditional bail? The grounds for doing so are circumscribed by the Bail Act; see page 124. If so, what conditions will most effectively achieve the purpose?

Other structures

Structures to guide magistrates in their thinking have also been devised to deal with mode of trial decisions; 'no case to answer' decisions; enforcement proceedings; and others. These are not dealt with in detail here, other than to note that they all adopt broadly the same approach of clarifying the questions to be answered and applying the relevant law. Mode of trial and 'no case to answer' are dealt with in Chapter 5; and enforcement in Chapter 9.

Deciding who and what to believe

All that has been said above about structured decisions helps magistrates identify the decisions they need to make. But it tells us little or nothing about which side to come down on when the evidence conflicts, is inconsistent, or plain muddled. In the absence of lie detectors and truth drugs (even if they are reliable), how do magistrates go about sorting the truth from the untruth, fact from fiction, reliable evidence from invention? Given that witnesses can misinterpret events, forget, elaborate and invent, intentionally or unintentionally, innocently or maliciously, how does the bench recognise misperceptions, errors and exaggerations? And how do magistrates decide how important each piece of evidence is relative to others? The remainder of this chapter sets out some ideas on how to distinguish lies from truth; spot mistakes; identify unreliable evidence; and how to attach varying degrees of weight to different elements of the evidence.

First, though, it is worth bearing in mind that many of the rules and regulations which bear on how trials and other proceedings are conducted are themselves designed to promote fairness and balance. A lawyer need not necessarily believe the case he or she is presenting, but is bound by professional rules which prohibit misleading the court. The rule against hearsay is intended to eliminate the possibility of putting before a court matters which cannot be tested. Leading questions are not allowed because they put words into the witness's mouth — words which might not otherwise have occurred to the witness. The rules about referring to notes to refresh memory require the notes to have been contemporaneous or nearly contemporaneous, again a precaution against being prompted by notes the accuracy of which may have been tainted by the passage of time. The purpose of cross-examination is to highlight inconsistencies and inaccuracies. All these are designed to ensure that the process itself is as conducive as possible to truth and accuracy, but there are clearly severe limits on what can be achieved by rules of this kind.

It is worth remembering, too, that apparent conflicts in evidence can sometimes be resolved by a question from the bench, although the magistrates should of course confine questions to clarifying the evidence which has been given; they should not introduce new matters or perspectives. Thus, for example, where the prosecution, in opening its case, referred to a blue car, but the prosecution witnesses referred to a green car, a question from the chairman of the magistrates produced the elucidation that, during the course of preparing the case, the word 'sapphire' had erroneously come to be used to describe the colour of the car; it was in fact the name of the model.

Motive

First, does the witness have a motive to lie? For a defendant, avoidance of conviction is an obvious motive. A friend of the defendant likewise may wish to cover up. A co-defendant may seek to place more blame on the other defendant(s). The victim of a crime may lie to encourage the conviction of the accused out of a misconceived sense of revenge. It has transpired, in a small number of high profile cases, that police officers have lied to secure convictions.

On the other hand, professional witnesses such as doctors are subject to professional rules and are less likely to be motivated to lie, and independent witnesses who have no direct interest in the case, again, are unlikely to have any reason to lie. But it is conceivable that a professional witness might exaggerate out of vanity or a desire to impress. And the evidence of an otherwise independent witness may be tainted by personal bias or prejudice, or the witness may, out of sympathy for a victim, unwittingly elaborate the evidence against the accused.

But motive alone is rarely definitive. A relative of the defendant may have acquittal as a motive for lying, but could equally well adopt the opposite standpoint — a responsible parent may wish justice to prevail, regardless of the consequences for his or her son or daughter. The reasons for lying or putting a slant on evidence are many and varied.

Attitude

The attitude of a witness — the way in which he or she gives evidence, also known as the witness's demeanour — makes a nebulous but sometimes important contribution to assessing the evidence. It comprises many aspects: how the witness is dressed; how he or she speaks, e.g., accent, tone, volume and clarity; whether any bias or hostility is displayed, e.g., in favour of the defendant, against the police in general, for or against members of a certain cultural group, and so on; body language, e.g., whether or not the witness meets the questioner's eye or looks away; whether the witness remains cool when challenged or becomes flustered. Where a witness gives evidence through an interpreter, the magistrates can see gesticulations, signs of distress and other visible manifestations of the witness's state of mind, but if they do not understand the language, they will not necessarily catch certain nuances of meaning or changes of intonation.

But what does all this mean? Unfortunately, there are few conclusions to be drawn. Many witnesses appear nervous or uncomfortable. This may be because they are lying and/or exaggerating — all the time or some of the time, or they may simply be overawed by the experience of being in court or embarrassed by the questions being put. Witnesses who appear calm, confident, consistent and articulate are not necessarily telling the truth: members of Her Majesty's Government and a former President of the United States have been found to have lied. A person who is slovenly in appearance or contemptuous in answering questions may not endear himself to the magistrates but is not necessarily telling less than the truth. If a defendant says he lives on income support yet comes to court in the latest designer wear, mobile phone in hand, he may look 'all wrong', but may still be truthful — it is certainly possible that he acquired these accoutrements of style before becoming unemployed, or that they were given to him by an indulgent and well-heeled girlfriend. A person may be hesitant because he is trying to remember what he said before so that his lies are consistent with each other; on the other hand, he may simply be searching his memory for the right answer, or may not quite have understood the question. A person may say he does not remember because he genuinely does not, or because it is to his advantage 'not to remember'. A young man, when asked 'Was Martin driving the car' counter-questioned 'Do I have to answer the question'. He was told yes, and confirmed that Martin had been driving. But the eyebrow-raising interjection could have meant 'Yes, Martin truly was driving the car and I really wish I didn't have to confirm it because Martin is my friend and he is in trouble'; or it could have meant 'I am reluctant to answer this question because in doing so I intend to tell a lie'.

And so again, attitude or demeanour alone does not add up to much, and can only go into the melting pot with everything else.

Realism and credibility

To turn to a more helpful way of gauging the accuracy of evidence, we can look at how realistic it is. First, is it consistent? If a witness says that at 10 pm he was drinking in the Dog and Duck, and later says that at that time he was in the Flounder and Firkin, both cannot be true. Is he lying or has he just confused the names of his two favourite pubs? Magistrates may be inclined to discount both versions.

Apart from inconsistency within what an individual witness says, there may be inconsistency between what two different witnesses say. One may have seen a man of over six feet tall coming out of the pub; another may have seen a short, fat man. Can they possibly both be referring to the same person? Is there any explanation for their having such differing perceptions? Is one right and one wrong, or are they both wrong? On the other hand, if a number of witnesses give evidence of a series of details, all in uncannily identical terms, consistency may militate against accepting the evidence. For example, if three witnesses, all of whom saw the person in question only fairly fleetingly, all say words to the effect that 'he was six feet tall, had a limp, wore spectacles, was bald, was wearing a black bomber jacket, blue jeans and trainers', the evidence may be almost too good to be true; is it realistic, bearing in mind the period of time for which the witnesses saw the person, that they all remembered exactly the same details, and so many of them?

If different witnesses give evidence about a sequence of events, they are more likely to be believed if the evidence as a whole hangs together, and even more so if the witnesses are independent of each other. A shopkeeper says a woman became abusive and threatened violence while in the shop; another witness says she was waiting at the bus stop outside the shop and saw a woman in the shop waving her arms around and heard her shouting; a third witness says she was almost knocked over in the shop doorway by a woman storming out in a rage. But, without further explanation, it would not have fitted together quite so neatly had the second witness said she had been looking in the shop window at the time and saw the defendant looking at the merchandise in a perfectly calm and ordinary way.

Weight to be given

The circumstances from which the witnesses's testimony arose may add to or reduce the weight which the court attaches to it. Thus the longer the period over which a witness observed a state of affairs, closeness to an incident, favourable light and weather at the time, all go to increase the likelihood that it is reliable. A fleeting glance in twilight will carry less weight than a half-minute observation in daylight. A qualified motor mechanic's version of the condition of a car may well carry more weight than that of the driver of the vehicle with which it collided.

The ability of the individual to observe and remember has a bearing; it is said that the old and weak are often favoured as victims, precisely because they are less capable than others of perceiving and remembering details about their assailants. By way of corollary, because the police are trained in observation and note-making, in this respect their evidence is likely to be relatively reliable.

Features of the event in question may also affect recollection. Thus the victim of a street robbery will probably remember vividly the tug as her shoulder bag was pulled away from her, but out of shock, and the speed with which the event happened, may have a far hazier recollection of how many boys were in the group of attackers; how old they might have been;

what they looked like; and what they were wearing. The witness may have been under the influence of drink or drugs at the relevant time and that impairment casts doubt on the witness's ability to remember correctly.

A lecturer on criminal law used to test his students by arranging to be called out of a lecture to take a telephone call; while out of the room he would change his tie. Very few students, when later asked to describe what their lecturer had been wearing, noticed the change.

Sometimes, sheer volume of numbers counts. Thus if three witnesses give evidence pointing in one direction, and one gives evidence to the opposite effect, the version given by the first witness and corroborated by the second and third is more likely to be accepted as long as it is realistic and credible.

Inferences from circumstantial evidence

Sometimes, circumstantial evidence — evidence of secondary but material matters which may lead to certain inferences — may have to be assessed to work out what conclusions can properly be drawn from it. Circumstantial evidence often has to be relied on if no one witnessed the offence itself, as where it was committed in darkness or away from any other person. The prosecutor may, for instance, be able to show that the accused was in the right place at the right time, and had the opportunity to commit the crime. But more will be needed to prove the offence, and so, if it can also be shown that the proceeds of the theft in question were found under the defendant's bed the next morning, the magistrates may well decide that he did indeed commit the theft, unless he comes up with some other plausible explanation for the booty under the bed.

Making up your mind

Looking at the various elements of deciding who and what to believe, and the relative importance of those parts of the evidence which are accepted, leads to no hard and fast rules about how to come to conclusions. It is only when the totality of the evidence is assessed, bearing in mind all the factors which go to render it credible and reliable, and all the factors which militate against its credibility and reliability, that an overall judgment can be reached. In assessing the complete picture, the undisputed facts often help interpret the disputed matters. And the magistrates will keep in mind that for a criminal case to succeed, the facts must be proved beyond reasonable doubt. If the magistrates are left with a reasonable doubt, they must resolve that doubt in favour of the defendant and acquit.

The more factors weighing in favour of trusting prosecution witnesses, and the greater the credibility of their evidence, the more likely it is that the defendant will be convicted. Suppose the prosecution has brought two independent witnesses and they both confirm what the police have said in the case, both give broadly consistent versions of the facts, and neither seems to have any axe to grind; the defendant and his witness, a friend from work, both say the defendant was somewhere else at the time, but are vague about quite where that 'somewhere else' was, and had not mentioned that the defendant was elsewhere until the trial. It is likely that the magistrates will find this case proved beyond reasonable doubt. On the other hand, if there is a single police witness whose version of events differs in some significant respect from that of the defendant — the defendant perhaps has some circumstantial evidence to back up his story, and the indications are that the defendant is trustworthy and that the police could be mistaken, the magistrates would probably be left with a doubt, and so find the defendant not guilty.

Another insight into how decision making is based on the totality of the evidence, using all the many and varied ways of interpreting it, can perhaps be gained from considering newspaper reports of cases. A newspaper report may give the impression that the sentence was too light or too severe. Of course, the sentence may not have been the most appropriate, but on the other hand the apparent anomaly may be explained by the fact that the reporter has missed out, whether deliberately or unwittingly, some essential element which weighed heavily with the magistrates or judge. Under the headline 'Holiday Maker Walks Free After Road Rage Attack', we may read a description of a vicious and inexplicable attack, but that the offender was only put on probation. We may or may not also read that there was also evidence of provocation, or that pre-sentence reports revealed significant mitigating features. Reporters do not necessarily absorb what they hear in the same way as do the magistrates; they may omit parts out of error or to sensationalise; the contents of a pre-sentence report are confidential and so not available to journalists. These possibilities not only make for caution in accepting at face value reports of cases which do not on the face of them 'stack up', but also illustrate the way in which courts take into account all the material factors in coming to a decision.

Eleven

Legal Aid

Introduction

Legal aid is a system of state funding for persons involved in legal proceedings who cannot afford to pay for a lawyer themselves. It is available to individuals only, not to limited companies or other artificial bodies. To be eligible for legal aid, a person has to qualify under two sets of criteria: one relating to the person's means; the other relating to the nature of the case. There are several kinds of legal aid, depending on the type of case. The most important for present purposes is criminal legal aid.

Solicitors and barristers are paid for legal aid work according to fixed scales, which are usually adjusted every financial year.

The legal aid system has attracted much criticism in recent years, notably because of the ever-increasing size of the annual bill to the state. In the financial year 1994/95, the total legal aid bill was £1.4 billion, double what it had been five years earlier. For their part, many solicitors believe they are not paid enough for legal aid work; and many individuals, particularly in civil cases, find themselves in the trap that they earn sufficient not to meet the financial criteria for legal aid, but not enough to pay their own legal fees.

Legal aid is regulated by the Legal Aid Act 1988 and by a host of statutory regulations made under the Act. In criminal legal aid cases, the court, applying certain statutory tests, decides whether or not legal aid will be granted. In civil cases, the decisions are usually made by the Legal

Aid Board, a government body established to act on behalf of the Lord Chancellor.

Decisions on legal aid can be made by either the magistrates or by the justices' clerk and staff; in most courts, they are left to officers of the court for the sake of efficiency and speed.

Legal advice and assistance

Under this scheme, which is also known as the 'green form' scheme, a solicitor can spend up to two hours (three in a family case) giving a person general advice, writing letters, negotiating and otherwise preparing a case. The applicant's capital and income must fall within certain limits to be eligible. Legal advice and assistance is given in many kinds of civil case, notably matrimonial matters, which do not concern magistrates, but it is also available to persons who are being questioned by the police, whether at a police station or elsewhere, and whether or not the person is under suspicion. Thus, witnesses and victims, as well as suspects, may be helped under this scheme.

Legal advice and assistance is administered by the Legal Aid Board and applications are made through the solicitor on, unsurprisingly, a green application form.

Assistance by way of representation

Assistance by way of representation, also known by the curious acronym ABWOR, is a scheme for providing for the costs of preparing a case and representing a client in certain proceedings. In the magistrates' courts, ABWOR is most commonly used in civil cases, such as proceedings for maintenance orders and certain matters under the Adoption Act. ABWOR is not available in proceedings under the Children Act; in these cases, civil legal aid may be available.

A magistrates' court may authorise ABWOR in civil cases for a person who is not otherwise represented if the court is satisfied that the case should proceed that day and if certain other conditions are met.

A magistrates' court may likewise grant ABWOR in criminal cases in certain circumstances of urgency to a person who is otherwise unrepresented and is, for example, applying for bail, or who is in custody and wishes to have the case concluded the same day. This is rare, and there are limits on the courts' powers. This type of ABWOR is not means tested, and the solicitor would apply for it in court.

If the police apply to the court for a warrant to detain a suspect beyond 36 hours, ABWOR is available to the suspect, and in these circumstances, again, it is not means tested.

Except where ABWOR is authorised by the court, an application must be made to the Legal Aid Board. The applicant's income and capital must be below the current limits and it must be shown that the applicant 'has reasonable grounds for taking, defending, or being a party to the proceedings'.

The duty solicitor scheme

Before the case comes to court

The duty solicitor scheme is organised by the Duty Solicitor Committee of the Legal Aid Board, in consultation with local law societies and regional committees. Magistrates, justices' clerks and police are among those who sit on the regional committees. It provides rapid, non-means tested advice to suspects and defendants in urgent need of it, either because they are being questioned by the police, or because they are before the court on a serious matter and do not already have a solicitor.

It has already been noted that people who are being questioned by the police about an offence, whether at a police station or elsewhere, whether or not they are suspects, and whether or not they have been charged, have a right to free legal advice. They may ask to consult a solicitor of their own choosing, a solicitor from the list kept by the police, or the duty solicitor. Whoever they choose, at this stage, legal aid is free and does not depend on the person's means.

To be included in the rota of duty solicitors, a solicitor has to meet certain requirements, relating mainly to experience, training, and proximity to the relevant police station(s).

A duty solicitor is available to suspects 24 hours a day. The solicitor on duty must accept a case referred by telephone, unless already engaged on another case; the solicitor must give advice to the suspect by telephone, or, if the solicitor is very near to the police station, must go there and give advice in person. If the suspect is drunk or violent, the solicitor can postpone giving advice, but must advise as soon as the suspect is capable. After giving initial advice, the solicitor must, in certain circumstances, for example where the suspect says he has been seriously maltreated by the police, go and see the suspect at the police station. Otherwise it is for the solicitor to decide whether it is in the interests of the suspect to go and see him or her at the police station.

At court

The regional committees decide, in consultation with local law societies and magistrates' courts, which courts should have duty solicitors in attendance and when, and make arrangements for duty solicitors to be available to defendants in courts where a duty solicitor is not routinely present at court. Some courts have a duty solicitor in attendance all the time, or mornings only, or on certain days only.

All defendants must be told that a duty solicitor is available. This is often done by means of notices in court reception areas, and/or leaflets given to defendants when they arrive at court. Often, magistrates themselves remind defendants that they may speak to the duty solicitor. This may be appropriate if the magistrates think a defendant is in need of advice, perhaps if a defendant is pleading guilty but it seems he or she may in fact have a defence, or is pleading guilty simply to 'get it over with'. Although the court may try and persuade a defendant to take advice, it may not of course require him or her to do so.

A defendant is not obliged to consult the duty solicitor of the day; indeed duty solicitors must tell defendants that they are entitled to instruct anyone they choose.

A duty solicitor at court is required to advise defendants in custody and to make a bail application if so requested by the defendant. The duty solicitor must also represent a defendant who is in custody on a plea of guilty if the defendant wishes the case to be concluded that day, unless the duty solicitor considers that the case should be adjourned in the interests of justice or in the defendant's interest. The duty solicitor must also advise and represent a defendant who is before the court for failing to pay a fine or other sum ordered on conviction, or for failing to obey an order of the court, if the defendant is at risk of imprisonment. The duty solicitor must also represent any other defendant if the solicitor believes the defendant needs it. Finally, duty solicitors must help defendants apply for legal aid for subsequent appearances.

While the services of the duty solicitor are available to someone at risk of imprisonment for non-payment of a fine 'or other financial penalty imposed on conviction', such as costs or compensation, they are not available to those at risk of imprisonment for non-payment of council tax. Indeed, although these people must be given the opportunity to take advice, no form of legal aid has so far been available, although a decision of the European Court of Human Rights in June 1996 is to the effect that it should be.

Duty solicitors may not, under the duty solicitor scheme, represent defendants in committal proceedings or on not guilty pleas; nor, normally, should they represent defendants accused of non-imprisonable offences.

Criminal legal aid

Criminal legal aid is available for criminal proceedings before a magistrates' court (including the youth court), the Crown Court, the Criminal Division of the Court of Appeal and certain other higher courts. It extends to preliminary appearances and bail applications as well as to trial and sentencing.

It is the court which decides whether or not to grant legal aid. The magistrates' court may grant legal aid for proceedings in its own court, and for Crown Court proceedings when committing a person there.

There are two tests for deciding whether or not to grant legal aid. The first is that it must appear 'to be desirable to do so in the interests of justice'. The Legal Aid Act provides that in making this decision, the court must take into account the following factors:

— the offence is such that if proved it is likely that the court would impose a sentence which would deprive the accused of his liberty or lead to loss of his livelihood or serious damage to his reputation;
— the determination of the case may involve consideration of a substantial question of law;
— the accused may be unable to understand the proceedings or to state his own case because of his inadequate knowledge of English, mental illness or other mental or physical disability;
— the nature of the defence is such as to involve the tracing and interviewing of witnesses or expert cross-examination of a witness for the prosecution;
— it is in the interests of someone other than the accused that the accused be represented.

Quite apart from these considerations, but subject to means, a person *must* be granted legal aid for certain matters. These include bail applications by people brought to court in custody and who are likely to be remanded or committed in custody; and sentencing a person who is to be remanded in custody for enquiries or reports to be made.

If there is a doubt about whether or not a person should be granted legal aid, the applicant must have the benefit of the doubt.

In the Preface to the 1993 edition of *The Legal Aid Handbook*, the then Chairman of the Legal Aid Board said:

> It is particularly important in legal aid that discretionary decisions are justifiable. Legal aid serves a number of stakeholders who may have conflicting interests, but each one has to be borne in mind when a decision is made. The stakeholders are the applicant, ... the legal adviser, the court and the Government (the taxpayer). What is the right decision for the applicant may not be right for the court or the taxpayer if legal aid is granted when it is unreasonable; what may be the right decision for the taxpayer may not be right for the applicant if legal aid is refused when it should be granted. The decision must be capable of being justified to the unsuccessful stakeholder in any particular case.

The Lord Chancellor's Department, the Legal Aid Board and the Justices' Clerks' Society have issued joint guidance on applying for and granting criminal legal aid. It quotes from a report published by the Legal Aid Board in 1992, which found:

(a) differences between courts in granting legal aid are attributable to the approaches of individual clerks;

(b) grants are more likely to be made according to court clerks' perception of the seriousness of the case, rather than according to the statutory criteria;

(c) applications for legal aid are often of poor quality, and the information provided to courts is frequently inadequate.

The guidance goes on to emphasise the importance of following the statutory criteria, and examines the 'interests of justice' criteria in some detail.

The application for legal aid may be made in writing by completing the appropriate form, or orally in court. In either case, legal aid cannot be granted until the applicant's means have been considered.

The application form requires the applicant to give personal details; to say what he is accused of doing; give the date of the next court appearance; and say whether any other criminal matters are pending. The applicant must also give reasons for wanting legal aid; the form sets out a number of possible reasons, based on the criteria for granting legal aid set out above.

A completed statement of means must accompany the application. In the statement of means, the applicant is required to set out all sources of income; his or her capital and savings; living expenses; and information about dependants. The statement of means must be supported by documentary evidence, such as pay slips, building society pass books, and a rent book. This is the basis of the second test of eligibility — financial means, which is based on both income and capital.

A defendant receiving income support, family credit or disability working allowance automatically qualifies for criminal legal aid and does not make a contribution towards it. Otherwise, from the information given in the application form, the applicant's disposable income and disposable capital are calculated in accordance with statutory rules, taking account of matters such as income tax, social security contributions, housing costs and the maintenance of dependants. The financial limits change from year to year, but for the year 1996/97, an applicant's disposable income must be below £49 a week, and his disposable capital below £3,000, to qualify for free criminal legal aid. If the disposable income is above £49, the person must contribute one third of the excess to the cost of the legal aid. If the disposable capital is over £3,000, the surplus over £3,000 must be used towards the legal costs. In June 1996, certain changes were introduced following public concern about the availability of legal aid to the apparently wealthy. There are now special rules applying, for example, to those having homes worth over £100,000 and to those who transfer capital assets to a family member or other person.

A solicitor cannot be paid for work done before legal aid has been granted unless the interests of justice required that the defendant be represented or advised urgently; the solicitor did not then unduly delay in applying for legal aid; and the work was done by the solicitor who is subsequently assigned under the grant of legal aid. For this reason, it is sometimes necessary to adjourn a case so that the defendant can apply for, or await the outcome of an application for, legal aid.

Civil legal aid

Civil legal aid is available for certain cases in the magistrates' courts. It is also available for proceedings in the county courts, the High Court, the

Court of Appeal and the House of Lords. Cases before certain tribunals, for example the Employment Appeal Tribunal, also qualify.

In the magistrates' courts, civil legal aid is most commonly used in cases under the Children Act 1989, although it is also available, for example, in certain adoption matters; and for enforcing maintenance orders made by courts overseas.

The application is made by the applicant's solicitor, to the Legal Aid Board. Usually (but subject to important exceptions in Children Act cases), the applicant must satisfy a means test and may be required to contribute towards the cost of legal aid. A person in receipt of income support automatically qualifies for civil legal aid, regardless of capital. Those whose income is below £2,498 a year qualify for civil legal aid without having to make a contribution; those whose income is between £2,498 and £7,403 a year qualify but must pay a contribution. The equivalent limits on capital are £3,000 and £6,750. The limits are slightly more generous in personal injury cases.

If an applicant satisfies the means test, then, as a general rule, civil legal aid will be granted only if the applicant can show reasonable grounds for taking, defending or being a party to the proceedings and that it is reasonable to take the proceedings. For example, civil legal aid would not be granted to fund proceedings in which money compensation is sought from a defendant who has no means of paying any judgment that may be given against him.

But in certain cases under the Children Act that test does not apply, and certain people are entitled to free civil legal aid regardless of means. Those people are the parents (including the unmarried father) of the child in question; the child; and those who have parental responsibility for the child. The cases in which free legal aid is available without means test are proceedings for care and supervision orders; child assessment orders; and emergency protection orders (including proceedings about the duration and discharge of emergency protection orders). Other parties to proceedings of these kinds, and people applying to be joined as parties to them (for example, grandparents, aunts or uncles), have to satisfy the means test, but not the 'reasonable grounds' test.

In addition, if an application is made to hold a child in secure accommodation, the child must always be granted civil legal aid regardless of means and regardless of the merits of the case.

In proceedings concerning education supervision orders, applications to discharge care orders and other public law proceedings, and in private law proceedings, the usual tests of means and reasonableness apply.

Legal aid is not available to local authorities and guardians ad litem in Children Act proceedings.

The rate for the job

Solicitors are paid by the Legal Aid Board for legal aid work in the magistrates' courts according to certain fixed scales and by applying statutory tests. Thus, the Board takes into account 'all the relevant circumstances of the case including the nature, importance, complexity or difficulty of the work and time involved ... and a reasonable amount is allowed in respect of all work actually and reasonably done'. The scales are generally revised upwards a few percentage points every year. Unsurprisingly, many solicitors say they are underpaid for what they do, while the Government seeks to contain the ever-increasing legal aid bill.

Rates of payment vary slightly according to whether or not the solicitor's firm is franchised by the Legal Aid Board, franchised firms receiving slightly more than non-franchised firms. The Board introduced the franchising scheme with the purpose of improving the service to clients. It has not been universally acclaimed by solicitors, some of whom say that far from improving the service, it has simply added to the bureaucratic burden. Rates also vary by location, solicitors in London being eligible for slightly more than those elsewhere.

For most criminal legal aid work in magistrates' court cases, standard fees per case apply. Cases are categorised according to complexity, more being paid for the more complex cases. There are also 'lower standard fees' which range from £144.25 to £602, and 'higher standard fees', of between £346.00 and £963.00. The amount paid is assessed by the Legal Aid Board, on the basis of the solicitor's claim, according to the costs of preparing the case, advocacy in court and a number of other matters. If a barrister has been instructed by the solicitor, without the specific prior authority of the Legal Aid Board, the barrister is paid out of the standard fee which the solicitor receives.

There are rules about what constitutes 'a case' so that, for example, if two charges are preferred together, only one standard fee is usually payable. If a solicitor acts for more than one defendant in the same proceedings, the standard fee covers all the defendants.

It was reported in The Law Society's *Gazette*, in May 1996, that, according to the Lord Chancellor's Department, the top 20 legal aid firms earned an average of about £2 million each in 1994/95. A London firm earned an exceptional £8.3 million in legal aid fees in 1994/95, although most of this related to a six-year civil case against British Nuclear Fuels in which it was unsuccessfully argued that the Sellafield Nuclear Reprocessing plant had caused leukaemia in children. The same report mentioned that a Gloucestershire firm, which had earned the highest legal aid fees in 1993/94 and the second highest the year following, was raided by police in January 1995 as part of a fraud investigation.

Proposals for reform

At the beginning of July 1996, the Government published a White Paper containing proposals for extensive revision of the legal aid system. The main purposes are said to be to seek better value for money spent; to use state funding to support only deserving cases; and to avoid certain injustices in civil cases concerning the winner's ability to recover the costs of the case from the loser.

The main features of the proposals are:

— cash limits on the overall amounts to be spent on criminal, family and civil legal aid;

— revisions to the way payments to lawyers are calculated;

— new sources of legally-aided advice, including citizens' advice bureaux and law centres and 'block contracts' with solicitors;

— almost everyone will have to pay something towards their legal costs;

— civil cases will have to be sufficiently 'deserving' to be eligible for legal aid;

— in criminal cases, those on benefits will be entitled to be represented at the police station and at their first court appearance without cost; everyone else will have to pay a fixed contribution; the 'interests of justice' test will remain unaltered; and contributions will be refunded if a defendant is acquitted.

The proposals will undoubtedly lead to much controversy and debate, and their future will depend largely on the political fortunes of the Government which introduced them.

Twelve

Life as a Magistrate

Introduction

Life as a magistrate brings with it certain individual and personal considerations, and makes considerable demands. Some of these, strangely, seem not to be widely aired elsewhere, although others are the stuff of training courses. In this chapter, an attempt is made to review some of these matters.

Open-mindedness

Much is said elsewhere about recognising prejudice and eliminating it from reactions to what is said and done in court and from decision-making. It need not be further elaborated here other than to reiterate that prejudice, personal predilection, and partiality are in direct opposition to the principles of simple fairness and open-mindedness with which magistrates approach their tasks. All are equal before the law, and in taking the judicial oath or affirmation, magistrates espouse this principle. New magistrates rapidly realise that they can listen to a prosecution case and find it entirely convincing, only to discover that, having then listened to the defence, the case has taken on an entirely different complexion. It is a simple truth that no one is in a position to make up his or her mind until they have heard both (or all, for there are often more than two) sides of the story.

Personal interest

Since justice must be as transparent as possible, there are times when, because of some personal circumstance, an individual magistrate should not participate in a case, since others may perceive that, whether or not it is in fact the case, he or she may not therefore be able to approach the case impartially. For example:

— the defendant is accused of illegally abstracting electricity and you own shares in the electricity company concerned;
— the defendant turns out to be someone you worked with some years ago, your son's girlfriend, or your next-door neighbour;
— the defendant is accused of making illegal video recordings; you work in the media and participate in industry discussions about stamping out this practice;
— the defendant is accused of stealing from his employer, X Co., a major national company. You too work for X Co., but at a different location from the defendant, and you have never seen or heard of the defendant.

In cases like this, sometimes only the magistrate concerned knows there is potential for conflict; the defendant may recognise the magistrate, but not necessarily realise its implications. It is up to the magistrate to volunteer that he or she has an interest, in the first place to colleagues. Once it is agreed that a magistrate should not sit on the case, an open announcement that the magistrate has disqualified himself or herself from the case is made. The case may then be moved to another court which is in session, or the magistrate in question may simply leave the court room while the matter is dealt with by the colleagues remaining.

Ignoring something

On the other hand, there are rare occasions when magistrates have to close their mind to something. Suppose a witness has made a remark in breach of the rule against hearsay and the bench has been asked by the legal advisor to ignore it. For example, 'I know he was there because my mum told me she saw him', and the witness's mum is not being called to give evidence. This may be a very revealing piece of information in the context of the evidence as a whole, but if the bench is told it is not admissible, they must accept that it is not and proceed as if it had not been said. This is in fact simpler than it might sound. The remark is omitted entirely from the steps in structured decision-making and so is afforded no weight or relevance. Put another way, it is simply a matter of imagining how the case would be viewed had that remark not been made at all, and proceeding on the basis of the information which remains. Experience confirms that is not nearly such a feat of mental gymnastics as might first appear.

Akin to this is the problem of a lawyer or witness whose manner or tone is irritating, pompous, arrogant, condescending, long-winded, repetitive, boring or plain silly. If a person is positively rude, the chairman may have to find some dignified and non-emotive words to request a modification of behaviour. When it comes to deliberations in the retiring room, the attitude of a witness may, as we have seen, be relevant when weighing that person's evidence, but that of the lawyers is another matter. It may be wise to walk up and down the corridor three times to dissipate anger, or (first taking care to be quite of earshot), laugh off the ill-effects. What is important is to distinguish reactions to the lawyer's behaviour from the evidence itself. It is not the defendant's fault if he has a low-grade lawyer, and he certainly should not suffer because his lawyer has an unfortunate manner. The same is true in reverse; articulateness, intelligence, elegance of argument, charm, good humour, and even good looks, do not of themselves enhance the quality of evidence.

Stressful cases

In the same way that prejudice is to be eliminated, so too emotional reactions must be identified and taken out. Often, what magistrates are told about defendants will arouse sympathy, as where the defendant was in dire poverty, or recently bereaved, or his wife had just left him for another man. While circumstances of this kind often temper the sentence, they rarely have a place in decisions about guilt or innocence. Most of the abjectly poor and those who endure tragic personal circumstances are nevertheless scrupulously honest; they too deserve justice.

Emotional reactions come in at another level and call for a measure of detachment familiar to those who work in the medical profession, and many other sectors. Cases may sometimes, although fortunately rarely, be distressing. Defendants suffering mental illness are probably the commonest example. At the extreme can be a case in the family proceedings court where, having carefully weighed all the evidence, the magistrates conclude there is insufficient evidence to make an emergency protection order. Forty-eight hours later the child in question is found dead and the parents have been arrested, suspected of having fatally injured her. This is indeed tragic, but magistrates need to be dispassionate. If they did their job properly, examining each piece of evidence, assigning weight, credibility and relevance to each, they will have confidence that the decision they made was the right one on the basis of the information they had. The family court is a court of law and must not speculate or try to look beyond the evidence before it. There may have been other evidence which could have been gathered and put to the court, but was not; that is a matter for the authority which brought the proceedings, not the magistrates. At the end of a court session, a magistrate should be able to come away with a degree of certainty that he or she has done the best that could have been done.

Appeals

Against that, however careful they are, magistrates can never be 100 per cent sure that they have got it right, which leads to the subject of appeals. Many decisions of magistrates are of course confirmed on appeal, but sometimes not. In most magistrates' courts there is a system for announcing the outcome of appeals. It may be disconcerting to learn that a decision has been overturned or the sentence adjusted (it may be even more disconcerting not to be able to remember the case at all!). An appeal to the Crown Court against a conviction in the magistrates' court is 'by way of rehearing', that is, the case is heard all over again without reference to what happened in the magistrates' court, except that the Crown Court may take into account inconsistencies between the evidence given in the magistrates' court and that given in the Crown Court. So it is possible that by the time a case is reheard, a crucial new piece of evidence has been found which leads to acquittal, or perhaps the defendant's lawyer has found a way of countering a piece of damning prosecution evidence.

Reports of appeal decisions usually come with a short note of the reason, which may or may not be enlightening, for example, a sentence may have been reduced at the Crown Court because the defendant gave many more details about his financial circumstances, leaving the magistrates wondering why this did not come out sooner.

The purpose of the right to appeal is of course to give redress to those who have been wrongly convicted or too harshly sentenced. Sometimes the only way to reconcile what the Crown Court decides with the conclusion the magistrates reached is to accept that the magistrates simply went wrong, perhaps misconstruing the evidence, not taking proper account of the guidance given by the legal advisor, or failing to take proper heed of mitigating circumstances.

Magistrates will always bear in mind the potential for errors, but should not be unduly undermined by having their decisions reversed; it is a strength of the system that convictions and sentences are susceptible to re-examination by others, and leads to the enhancement rather than the diminution of justice. 'The man who makes no mistakes does not usually make anything' is probably true — of women as well as of men — but the wise are careful to learn from their mistakes.

Work

Employers have long been required to allow magistrates time off work to perform their judicial duties. The most recent embodiment of this is in the Employment Rights Act 1996, which says that 'An employer shall permit an employee of his who is a justice of the peace to take time off during the employee's working hours for the purpose of performing any of the duties of his office'. It goes on to provide that 'An employee may present a complaint to an industrial tribunal that his employer has failed to permit him to take time off as required . . .'. But an employer is not required to pay an employee magistrate while at court, although some do, perhaps accepting in return extra unpaid work from the employee.

Employers vary considerably in their approaches to employee magistrates, some being very much more accommodating than others, perhaps taking the view that they should contribute to the justice system by freeing the employee, or wishing to 'reward' the employee, or even believing that a magistrate employee enhances the image of the company.

In view of general commercial 'downsizing' and its effects on the job market in recent years, these considerations are, if anything, more important than they used to be. No matter how helpful an employer wishes to be, the nature of some some types of business, the structure of certain organisations, market conditions and many other factors inevitably restrict the scope for flexibility.

The self-employed — and there are increasing numbers of them — generally enjoy greater freedom in planning their time, but are perhaps more likely to feel frustrated by losing time waiting for a case to start because the defendant, counsel or a witness is late, conscious that their own work is not progressing and that they will have to use what would otherwise be free time to catch up.

Allowances

Magistrates are entitled to claim travelling expenses. If a magistrate uses his or her own car or motor cycle, there is a 'per mile' allowance varying according to the engine size of the car; the rate reduces if more than 5,000 miles are claimed for. There are also subsistence allowances to cover the costs of meals for magistrates who are away from home for more than four hours; they vary from £5.70 to £15.00 according to the number of hours away. And there are certain allowances for loss of earnings; higher rates are paid to the self-employed who are subject to income tax on these payments.

Details of the current rates, and how to claim them, appear in most retiring rooms.

Dress

Not much need be said about how magistrates should dress, except that their clothes should accord with the neutrality of the office and should not include any items which could, even remotely, suggest bias or indicate individual views, such as club ties or political campaign badges. Like legal advisors and other lawyers appearing in court, magistrates should simply appear neat and dignified. Many people who work in the professions can simply wear their work clothes. Magistrates with limited means should not feel under any obligation to buy clothes specially to go to court, and should not worry if they have only one or two sets of clothes which are suitable. There is no pressure to follow fashion, and chain store clothes are perfectly acceptable.

Entrances and exits

Likewise, magistrates make their entrances and exits in a calm and quiet way. At the beginning of a session, the legal advisor will already have made his or her way into the court room before the magistrates. The chairman of the court usually agrees with colleagues in advance who will sit on the left and right, so they can enter in the appropriate order. If the chairs are awkwardly positioned and magistrates are unable immediately to get to their places (more likely in some cramped court rooms), it is wise for them simply to stop and move the chair; this is safer than risking the indignity of tripping! The same applies, obviously, when leaving.

Some magistrates seem to object to defendants having their hands in their pockets, but most agree that the magistrates themselves should not slouch, yawn, clean their spectacles, flick through books, or otherwise appear inattentive while in court.

Names and letters

It has already been noted that the terms 'magistrate' and 'justice of the peace' are generally interchangeable. In court, legal advisors and lawyers generally address them as 'Sir' or 'Madam'. Police officers seem to prefer the quainter 'Your Worship(s)', although most magistrates probably agree that the simpler 'Sir' or 'Madam' is a sufficient token of deference to the office they hold.

The use of the letters 'JP' seems to cause certain difficulties. Some magistrates avoid these difficulties altogether by never adding 'JP' after their names, but for those who wish to do so, the Lord Chancellor has given some guidance. The general principle is that the letters may be used, but not in circumstances which might give rise to any suggestion that the person does so to gain an advantage of any kind. The Lord Chancellor has said that even adding the letters 'JP' to personal notepaper can be taken to be an attempt to intimidate or impress, depending on circumstances and the relationship of the writer and the recipient; 'JP' must not appear on a driving licence, as a police officer, on stopping the driver, might see this as an attempt to influence the officer; nor should the fact that a person is a magistrate be mentioned in connection with a magistrate's candidature for parliamentary or local government elections.

There is also a convention about the order in which qualifications and awards are listed after a person's name. 'JP' is among the most important, since appointments to the office are made in the name of the Queen, and it therefore comes before, for example, university degrees.

The media

Since the work of the magistrates is of considerable local and national importance, it is unsurprising that members of the press or representatives of radio or TV stations may approach a magistrate for an interview of some kind. Again for reasons of preserving independence and neutrality, some care is needed when reacting to such an invitation. Since the fact of being a magistrate does not in itself restrict how a person may behave out of court, there is no reason in principle why a magistrate cannot participate in such an interview; particularly if it is no way connected with the fact that the person is a magistrate, as, for example, where it concerns a local arts festival in which the magistrate happens to be taking part, or what it is like to be one of the slowest runners in the London marathon. Nor is there any prohibition on magistrates giving talks to local groups about the work of the magistrate in general.

But in guidance given by the Lord Chancellor in 1988, he said that:

(a) Particular cases should not be discussed, and reasons for decisions should not be given unless the magistrates adjudicating gave reasons in open court, when it may be appropriate for the Clerk to repeat those reasons.

(b) The discussion that takes place in the retiring room is confidential and should not be revealed to anyone.

(c) It has to be recognised that journalists and others working for the media are frequently required to meet tight deadlines, but magistrates should not be panicked into making a hasty or ill-considered response.

(d) It is inappropriate for someone speaking in a judicial capacity to comment on government policy or on the policy of an opposition party or on other matters of public controversy....

The advice goes on to urge that if a magistrate is approached by the media, he or she should contact the chairman of the bench or the justices' clerk, who might be the better person to deal with it, and that any press statement should be cleared with the chairman. Both the Magistrates' Association and the Lord Chancellor's Department are more than willing to advise on these matters. Indeed, the Lord Chancellor went further in 1989, producing supplementary guidance on how magistrates should prepare for and conduct themselves in interviews.

The other side of the media coin is that the magistracy in general is often publicly criticised, perhaps for being out of touch, too stuffy, too severe, too lenient, comprised of unsuitable people, not representative, too old, too secretive, and so on. Because magistrates occupy public positions and their proceedings are public, and not least because what they do and say are matters of public concern, it is inevitable that they will sometimes attract criticism, and this should rarely cause any particular concern. Like many other groups of people in the public eye, it is the oddball and one-off events — the 'man bites dog' element — that attract attention, while most of the work that goes on invites no particular comment. Often criticism may be misconceived, perhaps being based on an incomplete picture of a case. Or there may be an answer to it — in Chapter 1 some of the reasons why the magistracy is still not, despite efforts, fully representative of the populations it serves have been examined. All in all, magistrates are probably wise to borrow from the media industry the view that bad publicity is better than no publicity!

Politics

What has been said above about communications with the media is of special relevance to those active in politics. Since magistrates must take scrupulous care that they cannot be seen as partial in any way, any public remark to the effect that, for example, the magistrate thinks a particular Criminal Justice Act is misconceived and should be repealed immediately jeopardises public perception of his or her neutrality in applying the laws in force.

This principle goes further, in that personal perceptions of the acceptability of particular pieces of legislation should not affect decisions made in court. An example *par excellence* of this was the poll tax (community charge). Many magistrates disapproved in principle of the way the tax was devised and levied, but nevertheless went about their part of the enforcement procedure in a perfectly neutral way. A magistrate who so strongly disapproves of a particular piece of legislation which impinges on their work in court that he or she cannot be neutral about it has little option but to resign from the bench; indeed he or she may well feel that that is an effective way of expressing the depth of their disapprobation.

Confidentiality

The deliberations of magistrates in the retiring room are of course private and should not be discussed with persons outside the court. They can be, and of course often are, discussed at length within the court, between magistrates who participated in the case and with other colleagues and with legal advisors; and perhaps in a bench meeting when considering the results of appeals.

Anything which has been said in open court should not give rise to problems if repeated or commented on elsewhere, although this does not of course apply to family and youth courts which are conducted in private.

Many documents read by magistrates are confidential and should not be discussed, or their contents disclosed, elsewhere. These include pre-sentence reports and statements and reports in family cases, which are now usually endorsed with an express statement of their confidential nature.

Legal cases

It has already been mentioned that the fact of being appointed a magistrate does not deprive a person of any civic right. Thus, sitting on the local bench does not prevent you suing the local store for having supplied faulty goods, or issuing a summons to recover an unpaid debt. But it is recommended that the magistrate tell the justices' clerk and the chairman of the bench what is going on. The same applies if a magistrate is a party to civil proceedings as a defendant.

Of far greater gravity would be where a magistrate is summonsed for, or charged with, a criminal offence. The magistrate should talk to the chairman of the bench and/or the justices' clerk without delay. It may mean refraining from taking part in any of the court's activities until the case has been determined, and it goes without saying that anyone convicted of a serious offence would be expected to resign from the bench immediately. Even fixed penalty notices (see Chapter 6) should be declared. The occasional parking ticket is unlikely to give rise to any real problem, but an accumulation of penalty points on a driving licence does not enhance the image of the magistracy and may well be viewed more seriously.

Personal difficulties

Occasional, short-term illness is unavoidable and can be dealt with simply by rearranging sittings or, in the worst case, cancelling a sitting at the last moment.

More long-term difficulties, such as impairment of sight or hearing which cannot satisfactorily be corrected, pose a greater problem and may lead a magistrate to have to consider whether or not he or she should continue on the bench.

Sudden illness during a session in court simply has to be dealt with in the best practical way possible. A magistrate who suddenly feels ill while sitting should simply ask for an immediate retirement in the hope of an equally rapid recovery, or, failing that, withdrawing from the day's proceedings.

Anecdotes about magistrates falling asleep abound; the prospect of this is a nightmare in more than one sense of the word. Magistrates can take obvious precautions — light meals without alcohol, for instance, but most are familiar with the occasional apparently interminable, repetitive and soporific speech from an advocate. A magistrate who feels in danger of giving way to sleep might ask for a short retirement — black coffee should help. A magistrate who thinks a colleague is becoming drowsy may also suggest a retirement or perhaps speak or pass a note to the victim.

A magistrate who is suffering from some particularly stressful personal circumstances, such as the long and grave illness of a spouse, may arrange to be relieved of sittings for a prolonged period.

Communications on the bench

Talking to colleagues while in court during a case can be difficult. Magistrates huddled together whispering is not conducive to the dignity of the court or, depending on the size and acoustics of the court room, to the confidentiality of deliberations. On the other hand, frequent retirements are costly in terms of time. Practice varies as to whether magistrates should communicate with each other orally or by notes.

In many cases it is obvious whether or not it is appropriate to retire; a retirement will usually be appropriate, for example, to read a pre-sentence report and decide sentence; or at the end of a trial, to decide guilt or innocence. In other cases it will be obvious that it is probably not necessary to retire — the decision to grant or refuse an adjournment, for example. The chairman will consult colleagues about whether or not they wish to retire, and it sometimes happens that, having first thought they did not need to retire, the magistrates soon realise that things are not as simple as first appeared, and change their minds. A magistrate, even if not the chairman, should not hesitate to ask for a retirement if it seems appropriate, as where he or she takes a different view from the others and wishes to talk it through.

In the retiring room

Tradition is that, although the chairman of the bench opens discussions in the retiring room, shaping the structure of a decision, he or she usually saves his or her opinion until last, allowing colleagues to put their views first. In Chapter 10, the process by which decisions are made was discussed at length. But what happens if the magistrates disagree? First, the use of an analytical, structured method, as we have seen, reduces the potential for conflict by eliminating extraneous matters which could give rise to disagreement and introducing a step-by-step approach which, at certain points, leads to inevitable, logical conclusions which are difficult to challenge. But what if colleagues take fundamentally different views of the significance of a particular piece of evidence, or of the credibility of a witness?

Those who are interested enough will find the libraries well-stocked with books by management gurus and psychologists on how to put arguments and win negotiating points; and for lawyers on how to put their cases convincingly. Much of what is said there may apply in the retiring room; for example, round tables are probably better than square ones since they discourage the confrontational element of sitting opposite someone with whom you may disagree. There are also a few points which perhaps apply particularly to magistrates.

Magistrates have a joint responsibility to find consensus, and they are 'on the same side' — the side of seeking the just outcome. 'We' is often a more neutral pronoun than 'I'; for example, 'yes, but if we come to that conclusion, does it take sufficient account of what witness X said?' rather than, 'you can't say that because you're ignoring what X said'. This is also an example of the benefit of putting a point by way of a question rather than a categoric statement; a question invites the hearer to consider the question; a statement may be more likely to invite a contradiction.

Humour may have a place too in keeping the heat out of a discussion, and can often be introduced without in any way compromising the gravity of the decision being made.

If the magistrates begin a discussion with different views, and end it with a consensus, then clearly someone must accept that they are wrong. Anything which makes this easier — allowing someone to 'save face' — facilitates the discussion. In the example above, the person apparently not taking account of the evidence of witness X may simply have forgotten about it, and can probably gracefully admit to having done so in response to the question. The other side of this coin is that in retiring room discussions, magistrates should never be afraid to back down when they realise they have misunderstood something or just got it wrong.

Of course, a bench of three magistrates, whether they have known each other for years or have only met that day, can often thrash out a difficult question on which they at first disagree without any risk of offending each other, and this is as it should be. All magistrates have different approaches and personalities and that is one of the strengths of the system. Discussing a difficult case is often absorbing and challenging, and finding agreement after a vigorous but courteous debate is one of the most satisfying aspects of the work.

More difficult may be the situation in which a magistrate strongly disapproves of some element of a colleague's behaviour. What if a magistrate makes a remark which a colleague believes displays prejudice, lack of neutrality or partisanship? Worse still, if the chairman makes such a remark in court?

A magistrate may need to muster some courage to deal with a situation like this and, since it goes to the heart of the system, should not let it go by. It may mean asking for an immediate retirement. A strong magistrate may be able to take a direct approach — 'Could what you said be taken to indicate bias? I am extremely worried that it might be interpreted that way?'. Or it may be wise to break off a retiring room discussion to speak to the most senior magistrate at court that day, or the justices' clerk, to express concern and seek guidance. In extreme cases, the bench disciplinary procedure will be invoked.

Disciplinary procedure

All benches have a procedure for dealing with complaints about magistrates, whether it be something said in court or in the retiring room, or about some aspect of their behaviour out of court. The complaint may be made by a fellow magistrate, a member of the staff, or indeed any member of the public. The chairman of the bench will consider the matter first, meeting the magistrate in question in private or with the clerk to the justices. The magistrate is given every opportunity to explain the conduct complained of. A note of the interview is sent to the advisory committee which appoints magistrates in the first place. In more serious cases, or if there has been more than one complaint, the matter may be dealt with by the advisory committee rather than by the chairman of the bench. Again, the advisory committee will probably want to talk to the magistrate, first notifying him or her of the nature of the complaint. And again, the magistrate will have the opportunity to explain himself or herself. In the worst case, the matter is referred to the Lord Chancellor, who may ask a magistrate to resign, or, ultimately, remove a magistrate.

Fortunately, this procedure is needed extremely rarely and is not a matter for concern for most magistrates.

On that rather serious note, this short review of some of the private concerns of magistrates comes to a close. In all cases of individual difficulty, a magistrate can turn to the chairman of the bench or the clerk to the justices, or even the Magistrates' Association or the Lord Chancellor's Department; there is a wealth of experience to draw on, and it will be rare that a particular problem has not cropped up before and an answer found. Serious difficulties are truly rare. For the most part, life as a magistrate is challenging, interesting and rewarding.

Index